Back to Basics

I have found that some small jewels are hidden inside small books like this one—processes, ideas, thought-provoking perspectives that make an impact on my agency operation and sometimes even incite major changes.

My desire as I write this book is to do just that. I hope you find many jewels in this book as together, we chart the course to a successful insurance agency.

Back to Basics

Charting the course to a successful insurance agency

Tony Fernandez

About the Author

Tony Fernandez was born in Spain and moved to the United States in 1993 with his wife, Lissa, and their two sons, Stefan and Chris.

He holds a Bachelor of Science in eCommerce from the University of Phoenix and graduated (summa cum laude) from Regis University with a Master of Business Administration in Marketing. Currently, Tony is considering several universities to pursue a doctorate in Business.

Currently, Tony is the president and chief executive officer for Affordable American Insurance, an independent insurance brokerage company.

Under his leadership, the company has maintained a consistent 30 percent growth in sales in the past few years. AAI has received multiple awards for being one of the top companies in the region for companies like Travelers, Safeco, The Hartford, and Kemper Insurance, to name only a few. In 2009, AAI was named one of the top one hundred privately owned companies in Colorado by *ColoradoBiz* magazine.

One of Tony and Lissa's passions is helping people in need. For the past decade, their family has traveled to the Dominican Republic. In one of their trips, they found out that one of the local families had lost their child to a sickness which could have been treated if the family had funds. Since then, Tony and Lissa have raised funds to send $1.5 million in medical supplies to the nation's children's hospital in Santo Domingo, capital of the Dominican Republic. The shipment set sail for the hospital in January

2010. When the Fernandez family arrived in the Dominican Republic to deliver the shipment, the island nation was being flooded with wounded people from Haiti, the neighboring nation that just three days before had suffered a devastating earthquake killing three hundred thousand people and wounding another three hundred thousand. When the world was starting to gather resources to send to Haiti and the Dominican Republic, the shipment with medications that the Fernandez family sent was already on the island and being used to help the wounded.

Tony is a member of Rotary International and an honorary recipient of the Paul Harris Fellow award. RI was the vehicle used to raise the funds and send the shipment with medical supplies to the Dominican Republic.

Tony's hobbies involve the outdoors. He loves his mountain bike in the summer and his skis in the winter.

Dedication

I want to dedicate this book to my family. My wife, Lissa, is my best friend and adventure partner from whom I draw strength and wisdom. My sons, Stefan and Chris, who are now adults, are in all my adventures and fun stories. Fun and abundant laughter are present in all the things we do together. Lissa and I are very proud of them. It is a great feeling as a parent to see your children become an asset to their community, their country and society.

Acknowledgments

I want to thank my wife, Lissa, for her support and input on the information provided in this book. She is the glue that holds me together. Lissa has worked very hard to educate herself in the insurance industry by obtaining the Certified Insurance Counselor (CIC) certification. The knowledge and the experience that she has have contributed directly and indirectly to the information of this book.

Barrett Bartels, a friend and partner, is a great sounding board for my business ideas and has the great ability to see my vision and break it down into steps so that it can become a reality. Barrett makes me a better leader. He has been instrumental in the information provided in this book.

Debbie Massey, who since this book was written has moved out of state, was my assistant when I was writing it. Her writing skills were very useful as she read and corrected my writing.

James Switzer, my good friend and family member (Lissa's cousin), is the vice president of corporate income for AAI. He is one of those unique individuals who are highly skilled in math and also in writing. These two skills rarely go together. Jim has been very instrumental in reading and correcting this book.

Shelly Patterson, my present assistant, has been very instrumental in coordinating the final steps to publishing this book. Her commitment and dedication to make my office successful is unparalleled.

My good friend and fellow Rotarian Mark Walker, a business executive and a very influential individual in our community, also read this book. His input as someone from outside the insurance industry was very valuable to me. I continue to learn from Mark how to be a better citizen and how to improve my people skills. He is truly a master.

I also want to thank my uncle, John Costo, for his love, support, and inspiration.

BACK TO BASICS

1. Why We Do What We Do   2

2. Laying the Foundation   12

3. Creating a Winning Team   54

4. The Three Cores   76

5. Forming Your Team   96

6. The Glue that Holds it Together   116

7. Managing Your Time   130

8. Administration   144

9. Marketing and Branding   152

10. Build and Manage Your Agency   166

11. Taking Your Agency to the Next Level   188

PREFACE

It has been my desire for a long time now to share with you my experience selling insurance, managing staff, providing customer service to our clients, and creating a structure in which it all works like a well-oiled machine. This book is more a compilation of ideas, mistakes, and successes that I have experienced during my journey as an insurance professional than a philosophical or theoretical treatise. I have waited so long to publish it because every time I read it, I notice how much I have learned since my last edit. I continue to find cause to update it, yet I also realize that it is unfair to continue to withhold the information just because I continue to learn through new experiences. That is why I have decided to get it to you now with a commitment to continue to update the content of this book as my journey continues.

You will notice that I've written this book as a letter from one friend to another. I was tempted to give the book to a professional writer who would say the same things, only more color-fully. I've decided against that approach be-cause I want to share these notes with you, my friend, in my simple way and with all the pas-sion that I have for this industry. Overediting may take away the warmth and perhaps dilute the message that I want to share with you. I am not a professional writer, but I know that we all enjoy a letter from a friend, especially if we know we will come away inspired to take ac-tion. Therefore, I am going to give you the book just as I wrote it, which is in its pure form.

The intended audience for this book is the insurance professional who, day to day, faces similar challenges from many different fronts: insurance carriers, customers, office employees, legislation that continues to change, and technology, to name only a few. In the midst of all this turbulence, we insurance agents still love this industry. It gives us the opportunity to help families, friends, and customers to get their lives back on track after an accident or other misfortune. In addition, we distribute products that everybody needs in our culture. No one can buy a car, purchase a home, or open a business without an insurance policy. You are the professional insurance agent next to others so that they can continue building their lives with a shield of protection. What a wonderful industry!

You have different experiences and lessons that you've learned. I want to learn from you as well. I have created a Web site, www.TheInsuranceProfession.com, where you can post brief notes on the things you learn from this book and how they hopefully help you improve your agency, or even personal anecdotes about your own life lessons that you might want to share with other insurance professionals around the nation. Many may wonder, "Why would I want to share my victories with other agents?" Unfortunately, that way of thinking has been one of the biggest mistakes we make in our business. That mentality has segregated our already fractured industry. We have paid a big price for it, and unless we change, it will cost us even more. We see, on a daily basis, outside industries offering insurance to their customers, which causes our agencies to lose business. I believe that we as insurance agents need to unify, share our ideas with each other, and raise the professional bar, thus making it more difficult for these outsiders to penetrate our industry and take our customers away.

CHAPTER 1

Why We Do What We Do

Anyone who lives within their means suffers from
a lack of imagination.

OSCAR WILDE

Irish dramatist and novelist

When I moved from Spain to Denver, Colorado, in 1993, I didn't know anything about insurance other than it was a product that would pay for a claim if I had an accident or misfortune of some sort.

My friend Ed Durnford introduced me to a multilevel marketing company, and after some research I signed a contract to sell their product. I was not familiar with multilevel marketing up to that point and paid close attention during the training provided by the company. The trainer and managers continued to refer to the insurance industry as one that pays over and over again residual income from a single sale. It wasn't long before I decided to pursue a career in the insurance industry as an agent.

I started my first agency selling health and life insurance, which I found fascinating. I watched my clients suffer through serious illnesses and found a sense of satisfaction as the insurance companies, through the concept of shared risk, paid the astronomical hospital and doctors' bills. The only things my clients were responsible for were the deductible and the co-payment. I remember an instance in which I walked into a store in Craig, Colorado. As I was speaking with the owner, attempting to sell him a health insurance plan, I found out that he was a diabetic and didn't have a health policy. Less than a year after he purchased a policy from me, he found himself in a hospital bed, waiting for an organ transplant. The hospital's and doctors' bills would have forced him into bankruptcy. He could have lost his business, his home, and everything he worked for all his life. Instead, he made a great recovery and, upon retiring, was able to pass his still-thriving business on to his son. If I had not walked into this gentleman's store that day, his life could have ended up much differently.

On another occasion, while I was review-ing the current coverages of a young couple,

I asked the husband if he had any form of life insurance that would protect his wife and daughters in the event that he experienced death prematurely. I went on to explain to him that a simple product like a term life insurance policy for twenty years would cost him a little more than fifty cents a day, the price of a can of soda pop. He agreed to submit an application, and within a short period of time the policy was issued. Six months later I received a phone call from the client's wife. He had passed away in a horrible car accident while driving home from Colorado Springs the night before. She was of course distraught and wanted to know what she needed to do to submit a claim. I can tell you that there is no greater feeling than the one I had a short while later when I went to her home to deliver the life insurance check. It was enough to pay off the mortgage as well as cover living expenses for at least a year while she put her life back together. Sitting in her living room, looking at her and her two small daughters, I realized that it was because of that day just six months ago, when I asked her husband that important question, that now she and the children would have a warm place and food on the table until she was able to get back on her feet. I occasionally wonder what would have happened to these people if I hadn't become an insurance agent, or, even worse, if I had missed the opportunity to ask the right questions in order to find their true needs. We, as insurance agents, have a lot of responsibility and the opportunity to make a huge impact on people's lives in the aftermath of the unforeseen.

These two stories are just a small sample of what keeps me motivated and excited about my chosen profession. Those of you who have been in the insurance industry for some time will have similar stories to tell, and I'd appreciate your taking the time to post them on my Web site to encourage all of us. There is no other industry like insurance, and I am very proud to be a part of it. I can't think of another job that offers such satisfaction…in addition to unlimited income! We are able to help people during the darkest hours of their lives, to be there with them through the process, and to become a part of their lives as they rebuild their future.

Another fascinating thing you may have already observed about being an insurance agent is that there is no industry like ours that enables you to make so many new friends. "My clients are my friends, and my friends are my clients" is not a cliché; it's very often the truth. To see the difference between our industry and others, let's compare it to the profession of selling widgets. The moment you have sold a widget to your prospect, the transaction is finished and you are unemployed again until you sell the next widget. If you want to develop a relationship with your prospect, you have to work very hard at it. The prospect offers resistance to your relationship because he knows that ultimately the only thing you are interested in is selling him an upgraded widget.

In the insurance industry we sell a sense of well-being. When a prospect buys a policy from us, he is not paying for a piece of paper; he is paying for a product that will be there for him in the event of a difficult incident or accident. He trusts that you have explained the different options so that the correct coverages are in place to protect him and his family. When he makes his payment every month, he does so with gratitude for your guidance and expertise. He expects that at some point in the future, if an accident occurs and a claim is made, you will have the chance to demonstrate why you were selected over your competition. The quality of your customer service, your expertise, and your professionalism are there when he needs you most. He will not forget how his *agent/ friend* helped him through his time of need, and he will show it to you by continuing to bring you a check for many more years to come and to refer your agency to his relatives and friends.

Many of us who have been in the insurance industry for years take for granted the fact that our customers continue to think of us every month and bring us a check to continue to pay for a product that we sold to them many years ago. I'm sure your Realtor friends or your mortgage broker friends would love to see their customers continue to come to their offices with a monthly check for the services that they provided years ago. Along with their monthly payments (premiums) comes your responsibility to review their coverages at least once a year.

In order to put things in perspective, let's continue to compare the insurance industry with other industries. This time we'll compare ourselves with the owner of a manufacturing company who wants to double his income every year. In order to do that, he has to continue to double his production of widgets, which includes a capital investment in machinery, raw materials, labor, and manufacturing space. Every year, in order to double his income, he has to buy more machines, hire more people, and expand his manufacturing space. He most likely would also need a large budget for advertising in order to create a greater demand for his product. How long can he maintain this growth?

Now picture your insurance agency. If you select the correct customers and treat them well, and if you work the same amount of time every year with steady production, your customer base may continue to double every year. As your customer base increases, you will have to hire more customer service employees, but you will not have to make large capital investments every year to maintain a phenomenal growth in income. You can double your sales every year while maintaining a fairly constant overhead expense. How many *legal* businesses do you know that can potentially double their income every year while maintaining fixed costs?

So we agree, the insurance business provides gratification on every level. We provide protection for our clients, we make our clients our friends, and our income potential is unlimited. As you read this book, I will continue to show you the uniqueness of the insurance industry and hope I can transfer my excitement to you to be a part of this profession if you're not already, and to thrive in the industry if you are already in it. I feel the need to do that because I've witnessed many agents and agency owners lose their passion for our profession. I hope to help them regain it and to keep others from burning out. The rest of this book will focus on how to build a strong, solid, well-planned, successful, profitable, pleasant, and consistent insurance agency...in other words, a well-oiled machine.

CHAPTER 2

Laying the Foundation

(Finding your DNA)

An expert is a person who has made all the mistakes that can be made in a very narrow field.

NIELS BOHR

Danish physicist and Nobel Prize winner

If you are new to the industry, the purpose of this chapter is to define the direction of your agency before

you add speed (adding clients to your book of business). If you don't point your agency in the right direction before you start writing policies, you may eventually find that you have built a book of clients that do not represent the agency that you had hoped to build. This chapter will help you establish a "north" on the "compass" of your business. If you are an experienced insurance agent, this chapter will help you find a fresh perspective while building your agency. It is never too late to fine-tune your direction if you believe that you've veered from your original course.

I have visited and interviewed many insurance agencies throughout the United States. It is not uncommon for an agency to grow and expand into several locations *accidentally*. This is what I consider an explosion. You, as an agency owner in the independent world, obtain a master code with several insurance carriers. Another insurance agent or licensed producer knocks on your door and asks if she can produce under your master code. She would like to represent the same companies that you have in your portfolio but cannot obtain a master code as an individual. Before you know it, you have experienced an explosion, with several agencies producing under you. What they do affects your appointment with the insurance carriers, positively or negatively. You find yourself in a position in which *you* have to manage the quality of *their* production.

In the direct writer world, the explosion happens in a more controlled environment. As a captive agent, you start your agency trying to sell as many policies as possible. Then, as you continue your growth through the first few years in the industry, you become amazed that new clients continue to come to your agency without your having to do much marketing at all, until one day you find yourself in an office managing four employees with personnel issues, payroll issues, needing more office space and a more sophisticated phone system to handle the volume of calls, etc. You have experienced an explosion.

When an explosion happens, it is uncontrolled and unplanned, and what looked like a good thing in the beginning could easily turn into a bad situation if you're not prepared. Let me give you an illustration to put this in perspective. You build a ranch home for your family. Then your in-laws have to move in with you, and you decide to build another floor for them on top of the ground floor. Then your best friends move to your city from out of town and ask if you could build another floor for them. Next, your sister and her family go through a bad financial situation and would like for you to build another floor for them. It was a great thing that you were able to help your in-laws, your friends, and your sister. However, since you only built the foundation for a one-story ranch home, the addition of the unplanned levels will eventually cause the whole house to collapse. This is inevitably the result of unmanaged growth.

In order to build a four-story building that is strong and safe, you must carefully plan for it, design it, and build the foundation strong enough and deep enough to handle the growth. The same is true for the growth of your agency. In this chapter, we will be asking a series of questions that will help you identify what type of agency you would like to build, how big you want to grow, and what type of customers you would like to serve. We will clear together a path that will enable you to walk through every day to reach your predetermined destination. When others see that you are growing, and you hear comments like "you are really exploding," you will know that what they are really witnessing is *managed* growth.

The first step is to find out what I call the DNA of your agency. You must know what your agency will be made of. You must identify your philosophy and establish your procedures. In order to be effective, set aside some time when you can be alone and give some thought to these questions. It is very important that you answer truthfully for yourself and not the way that you think others would want you to answer them. This is *your* business, and you have control of its destiny. There is no right or wrong answer. I am going to take some time to explain the questions. At the end of the section you will find all of the questions with the choices for you to circle or write in your answers.

Executive Vision

The vision for your agency is the DESTINATION to which you are going to take your business. Many of us don't see that very clearly. Let me give you an example. If you and I are talking about going on a vacation together with our families, and you are going to lead us on the trip, you need to sell me on a certain destination. Think about how you would sell me on your favorite vacation place. You would tell me where it is, the details of the hotel where we will be staying, what we will do every day we are there, and why we should pick that place. You would get excited about where we are going.

Think about this scenario. First, the destination is clear. You can visualize what the place looks like, and the fun activities and places we will visit get you excited. Why don't we do the same with our businesses? When I ask other insurance agents about the vision for their agency, they tell me that their vision is to provide excellent customer service. Is that a destination? What measures do you have in place to know when you have arrived there?

What is the experience of excellent customer service going to feel like? How do you do it (answer every phone call with a live voice, or help them with a claim, etc.)? Why did you pick that destination? Why are you excited about that destination? Remember, with our vacation, the destination was clear (we knew when we had arrived there). You visualized what the place was like and got me excited about going there; you explained to me with details of the activities what we were going to do each day.

Currently, I have the privilege to manage several insurance agents and their agencies. When we started working together, we spent time looking at the destination, getting excited about how we were going to get there, discussing the details of the processes, and brainstorming how the vision would be communicated to the staff and clients, as well as how we would know when we had arrived at the destination.

When we fly from Denver to Chicago, our pilot is very clear about the destination. He may have to make changes in the route due to wind direction changes, but the destination is clear and doesn't change. The same is true for our business plan. As we evaluate yearly how to fine-tune our processes and learn from our experiences, the destination stays the same. However, the most important thing is that we KNOW WHERE we are going and that we can get others excited about our destination.

Let's get started. First, we are going to deal with the **DIRECTION** of your agency. Do you want an agency that is going to continue to grow at a managed pace forever? Or do you want to reach a certain number of policies and plateau? There is nothing wrong with either of these scenarios. You may want to build a large business that you can hand down to your children. Or you may have other interests or hobbies and you would like to build an agency that becomes profitable enough to help you pursue your other goals while supporting your family. You must know what path you are going to take, because the structure for every agency is different in nature. For example, if your goal is to reach three thousand policies and maintain just those clients, the space that you would need for your operation would be room for a small customer waiting area, your office, and an assistant's desk. However, if your plan is to never stop growing, when you sign a five-year lease you are going to need to consider how much you want to grow in those five years, the number of employees that you hope to have, whether you'll need a conference room, etc.

The next question we need to ask ourselves is how we are going to **EXPAND**. Are you going to expand your business by acquisition or grow it from within? If you are very ambitious and your growth goals are bigger than what your agency can produce, then you are going to be looking for other books of business that you can purchase. Once you have established your philosophy by considering these questions, you will be able to identify the correct books of business that will be a good fit for your profile. Some direct-writer agents have a choice to expand by acquisition of other agencies, and other agents can expand by transfers.

The next question deals with **LEGACY**. Do you want to build a business that you can sell in the future or one that you plan to manage and give to your children? The way you answer this is going to reveal the set of lenses through which you will be looking at your business every day and how you will be making your business decisions. For instance, if you plan to sell your book of business in five years, you will take that into consideration when you sign a lease for office space. If you purchase another book of business, you will take into consideration how long it would take you to bring stability to that book so that the numbers show profitability.

Now we need to deal with the **FOCUS** of your business. Focus is of utmost importance in order to make an impact in the industry. In the business world, it is proven that when you focus on a type of service or product, you have the chance to become a leader in the industry. In the late 1980s, it was customary for large corporations to purchase other businesses that would be in their line of distribution. For instance, companies that were in the telecommunications industry providing the access line would purchase other companies that manufactured the phones. These companies eventually found out that they had lost their focus. When that happened, they also lost strength in their reputation, and some of them even lost their leadership in the industry. When once-loyal customers saw a particular logo on several products, they lost their faith and understanding of who the company was and its area of expertise.

Your prospects like to buy from an agent they view as knowledgeable and with a reputation in the industry. Your reputation is key to your success. To answer this question, you must admit that nobody can be an expert at everything. In the insurance industry, we have several areas in which we can become experts. There are personal lines, commercial lines, and financial services (in which I include health and life insurance products, annuities, and long-term care). Any one of these areas demands a great deal of knowledge and product updates; therefore, it is not possible to know it all. Your clients will also perceive the area in which you are an expert and will buy from you because they trust you.

As you consider your focus, you must also take into consideration the branding of your company. Select your business name according to your focus. It may cost you a lot of money in lost revenue if you become a generalist selling every line of business, unless you have producing agents in your office that are experts at different lines of business. Your clients must associate the name of your business with the product in which you are an expert. If you ask someone about the name Geico, they will tell you that it is auto insurance. You want a prospect to hear the name of your company and immediately know the line of business in which you are an authority. If you select personal lines as your focus and would like to expand to commercial lines, I would suggest that you hire a dedicated agent that knows commercial lines in-depth and perhaps even consider using a separate company name or DBA ("Doing Business As") to market that line of business. If you represent a captive company, hire licensed producers for every line of business and market their expertise.

You can visit www.TheInsuranceProfession.com and download the **Executive Vision document**. It will be an instrumental tool for you to visualize your choices and map a path for your agency.

Customer Service/Sales Employees

Now, let's address employees. I believe that it is better to find your style and beliefs before you start hiring employees and then letting them go because they don't fit your style and direction. In chapter 5 we will cover hiring techniques, how to interview prospective employees, how to hear what they aren't telling you, where to find them, etc. But for now you need to find your style and beliefs about your employees. Many agency owners find it difficult to answer the following questions.

The first thing that you must determine is how you are going to **COMPENSATE** your employees. What is your wage schedule going to be, below average, competitive, or above average? Companies like Walmart and McDonald's know that their turnover rate is going to be high; therefore, they usually pay their employees less than the competition. The key is the system with which they can train someone in a short period of time. Some insurance agents have a high turnover rate as a result of paying less than the competition. There is nothing wrong with this method of hiring employees, but you must develop a system with which you can train new employees in a short period of time to make them productive right away, as you're likely to face a high turnover rate.

Another option is to pay them a fair and competitive wage that will reduce turnover; however, I would still recommend that you institute a system to train employees in as short a period of time as possible. You can accomplish this by identifying the area in which you need the most help. Many agents hire employees, put them in a proverbial canoe, and tell them that the waterfall is very close so they must paddle upstream very rapidly to avoid a painful crash. If you find that your new employees leave you within the first three months of employment, you are probably doing this. Don't worry; we will address this later on in the book.

Always keep in mind that a new employee cannot learn the first week on the job what took you months or years to learn. Evaluate the workload that you have planned for this employee, select the area in which you need him most, and train him only in that area. One of the biggest fears that a new employee has is the length of time the training process will take before they can feel confident and useful. When employees feel needed and secure, they are much less likely to seek those things out elsewhere. You must limit their insecurity by shortening the learning curve as much as possible. You can accomplish this by training your new employees on one thing at a time until they have mastered each task. We will also explore this more in chapter 5.

You can also choose to pay higher than the industry standard in an effort to further minimize the turnover rate. I know several agents that have implemented this option because they got tired of training new employees. Not a bad method if you can afford it. The challenge is knowing in advance that the candidate is a good fit for your business and worth top dollar.

A combination of methods is also a good strategy: for instance, an entry-level lower pay for a receptionist; a better level of pay for an account manager with extended training; a better level of pay still for an agency manager. This also provides a promotion progression within the agency.

The next question is related to your method of **TRAINING**. The three choices are OJT (on-the-job training), an outside source, or mandatory systematic I work. On-the-job training simply means having your employees show up for their first day on the job and get to work. They may shadow another employee or be given a brief job description, but basically they are given room to learn by trial and error until they reach a level of proficiency. An outside source, whether it be specialized classes provided by insurance carriers or one-day seminars, can be beneficial, but these programs are rather generic and of course not specific to your agency's culture. In my opinion, a mandatory systematic training system is preferable. It is a less painful and more efficient method by which to bring your staff up to speed with less trial and much less error. This requires some forethought and preparation as you develop step-by-step procedures for training in the areas you want mastered. If you're hiring someone to answer the phone and open the mail, OJT is probably fine. If you have a part-time employee that is responsible for paying your bills and keeping your books, sending him or her to a class on QuickBooks or an advanced Excel course is a good idea. If you are bringing on an assistant who will do quoting and entering data into your agency management system, it would be best to train him or her correctly and thoroughly from the start. Being prepared for your new employee on day one will benefit both of you in the long run.

The next thing you need to consider is your **LICENSING** requirements. Will you insist that each employee be licensed or not? If you can run your operation with one or two employees, you should probably have them licensed. The natural implication is that if they are good employees and you want to keep them, you are going to have to pay them higher wages if they are licensed than if they aren't. A licensed assistant will most likely want a percentage of the commission that he is helping to generate.

Early on I had an unlicensed assistant that was doing an excellent job for my agency. Eventually I suggested that she get her insurance license so that she would have the ability to discuss coverages and such with my clients. After she got licensed, some of her working dynamic changed and I could tell that she had developed a more demanding attitude. Since I could not afford to pay her more at that time, she ended up leaving my agency to work for a larger organization. So if you are going to have your assistant licensed, be prepared to pay more if you want to keep them. If you have a larger operation, there are many jobs in your organization that do not need a licensed employee.

Once your agency has two or more staff members, you need to have a good handle on the **TASKS** that need to be performed daily, weekly, monthly, and annually. Do you want your employees to multitask or work in one specific area? If you have a two-person operation, you obviously each have to multitask. There is simply too much to be done. If your operation is larger, I would suggest that you consider having your employees dedicate their efforts in specific areas. You can train your customers to go to the correct employee for the specific service that they need. For instance, you might have a customer service employee and an employee that specializes in billing. When you have new clients, you need to introduce them to each employee and indicate his or her area of expertise, encouraging the clients to call the expert employee directly. Include your employees' business cards in the welcome package for new clients. This will save you time and allow everyone to work more efficiently. This is what I call "introducing your clients to your agency's culture."

You can visit www.TheInsuranceProfession. com and download the **Executive Vision**

document. It will be an instrumental tool for you to visualize your choices and map a path for your agency.

Agencies

Another area that you must consider in laying the correct foundation for the growth of your business is the **SIZE** that you want your agency to become. Let's define the three categories. A *small* agency has one or two employees; a *medium*-sized agency would have three to five employees; and I'd consider an agency with six or more employees a large agency. The larger the employee base, the more human resource issues you will need to consider.

It is critical that you decide in advance the size that you want your agency to become. As the leader, you must know where you are heading or you'll never know when you've arrived. If you want your agency to be large, you must learn how to operate at a CEO level before you get there, not after. If you decide to have a medium to a large agency, you may want to consider having an office manager who can cover for you when you are away from the office, as well as help you manage your employees on a daily basis.

As far as **RECRUITMENT** goes, will you be looking for experienced or inexperienced people? Either could work depending on your expectations. If you hire experienced people, you may have to pay them more, as well as correcting bad habits that they could have developed over time. If you hire inexperienced people, you can probably start them at an entry-level wage and be able to train them in the industry and in your agency's philosophy and procedures. In making this decision, you must also commit to thoroughly training employees new to the industry, since most errors-and-omissions claims come from agency employees, not the agent.

You can visit www.TheInsuranceProfession. com and download the **Executive Vision document**. It will be an instrumental tool for you to visualize your choices and map a path for your agency.

PROCEDURES

We are moving right along in the quest to find your agency's DNA. You must now decide how your agency is going to deal with **claims**. It seems like a simple question, but if you don't decide now and make clear to your team your method of following up on claims, you won't be ready when that critical moment arrives. I am going to take a bit of time with this section since, in my opinion, it is one of the most important aspects of our business. How we handle claims can either make or break us.

How important is *claims follow-up* in your agency? You can either ignore them since the carrier's claims department is handling it and wait for your customers to call if they have a problem, or you can take advantage of this opportunity and hold their hand through the entire process.

When I speak with clients, I hear that the single most important thing that they remember about an agent is how he handled their claim. I must say that the client remembers not only you as his agent, but also how the carrier's claims department and adjuster handled it. You must remember that the client selected *your agency*. The insurance carrier selected its adjuster for the client. The client has no choice picking an adjuster that he or she likes. To complicate matters more, carriers may subcontract the adjustment process. This may result in adjusters who not only do not represent your quality of service, but in many instances they may not even represent the quality of service of the carrier. What I am trying to express is that because they selected *you* from many agents available, the client expects more of you than of the adjuster.

As agents, claims are bad news. They affect our profitability which then may have a negative impact on our compensation. However, if you properly pre-underwrite the property and the vehicles, once a customer is in your books you must change your perception of claims. You need to act in his or her best interest and not your own; you want to advocate for him or her now more than ever. I hear from agents all the time, "I knew that this client would bring me trouble." Well, then...why put that prospect into your book of clients? If you don't filter your clients well, your attitude towards claims is going to be negative. You may find yourself bitter at them for making a claim at all. Avoid finding yourself in that situation by pre-screening, listening to your gut, and only taking on clients for whom you are willing to go to bat.

If all of your clients have been carefully selected, helping them through the claims process should be your number one priority. If you handle it well, your client will never want to leave you and of course will talk about you and your agency's excellent service to his or her family and friends. That is what I call "marketing with a claim." Just by your being there for them when help is most needed, your client will become your marketing arm. What I have done in the past with great success is, after holding the client's hand until the claim is paid, I call and ask if there is something we could have done better. If the client is satisfied, I then ask if she has family or friends that would like to experience the same level of service. In other words, I ask for a referral. I then mail the client a letter enclosing a self-addressed, stamped envelope, and I ask her to write a short recommendation that I can use in future printed marketing for my agency. By this I accomplish two things: I am asking them to write down the line that they will use when they talk about my agency with their friends and family, and at the same time I am getting their permission to publish the recommendation in my promos.

As insurance agents, we have the privilege of assisting people at the most vulnerable times of their lives: when their house burns down along with a lifetime of memories; when their teenager is in an accident and in the hospital; when a pipe freezes and water ruins their personal items and collectibles. When they make that frantic call to your office, they want to speak to someone who will make them feel secure and who gives them assurance that everything is going to be okay. When your clients are under extreme stress, they will remember your words forever. In the same way, a person remembers the doctor's exact words of comfort after they have been diagnosed with an illness. We as insurance agents may not realize the magnitude of the influence we have on our clients when a claim occurs. We have a chance to impact them either positively or negatively.

I am going to suggest that you make a priority of putting a claims procedure in place detailing how you and your staff are going to handle the entire process on behalf of your client. You may consider having one person that is dedicated to claims in your agency, preferably someone who is patient and pleasant and has the ability to make your customers feel that your agency is going to personally walk them through their claim. Remember that if you handle it professionally and with a high level of service, it will be your most cost-effective method of retaining current clients and bringing in more.

This brings us immediately to an important area in which you can improve your retention. Do you have a procedure in place detailing how your agency will handle **lapses**? As you know, a lapse is when a client doesn't make a payment on time, and even though they are still covered by their policy, it will cancel in a few days if they don't make that payment. You can ignore your client's lapses and hope for the best, or you can take the initiative and call your client, offering to take a payment over the phone in order to avoid cancellation.

Calling your clients when their policies lapse can be cumbersome and time consuming, but it is necessary in order to increase your retention by a few percentage points. I've noticed that lapses come more frequently from clients who prefer to make cash payment in person, but it also happens with clients that pay by EFT (electronic funds transfer). For example, they may have had a family issue and have forgotten to ensure the necessary funds are in their account to pay for their insurance. If your agency is going to accept clients that pay in cash every month, most likely you will have to have a dedicated person that calls the lapses *every day*. I must also mention that in order to avoid discrimination, unless you have a specific procedure in place, once you call a client, you must call *all* of your clients *all* the time. If you forget to call once, and the client lapses and has a claim, he could potentially take you to court since you didn't call to remind him of his payment; therefore, the court may deem it your fault that he lost his insurance coverage. If you don't have a procedure in place, you may involuntarily train your clients to wait until you call every month to come in and pay. One procedure I have seen work very well is to call the same client up to three times during a twelve-month period when their policy lapses. You will need to document each call in your Agency Management System so you will have a record in the client's file. When you have to call the client a second time, you will inform him that you will only call one more time, along with explaining the importance of keeping insurance payments up to date. As long as you document your conversations and still, after three calls, the policy cancels for nonpayment, you should not be responsible, since you informed your client of your agency procedures.

One way to minimize lapses is to strive to have all of your clients make their payments via EFT. I had an instance in which a client's family member passed away. She always came to the office to pay cash for her insurance. Due to the family emergency, she had to leave town shortly before her payment was due. Her insurance went into a lapse and I wasn't able to contact her. The inevitable cancellation was just more bad news when she got home. I use her story to demonstrate to new customers why EFT is the best way to make their payments. These days most people direct-deposit their paychecks and have overdraft protection in place, which makes it much less likely that their insurance would ever lapse, even during adverse circumstances.

The next question deals with **customer service** procedures; your choices are either having your staff handle all of your customer service calls or rerouting those calls to the insurance carrier's customer service centers. The latter may not be available to many of you, depending on the companies that you represent. There are benefits to each option. Handling basic customer service calls in house can be as advantageous as handling claims, i.e., a chance to assist and remind your clients why they chose your agency. The downside is it takes valuable time, and because these calls are more mundane in nature, letting someone else handle them shouldn't cast a bad light on you. The advantage of explaining to your clients in advance that they can call the carrier directly for a majority of their questions is that they get an expert on the line immediately. This is a plus for your client, but potentially a missed opportunity to connect for the agent. This method is fine as long as you maintain contact with your clients in other ways throughout the year. The client is usually going to be happy to call the customer service centers if they know that you are there for them in a real emergency.

Regarding **advertising**, are you going to depend on corporate advertising, or is your agency going to aggressively advertise for new prospects? Many of you may think you can only advertise if you have extra funds available. If you think that way, I would ask you to reconsider your marketing strategy. Successful businesses invest between 5 percent and 10 percent of their income into advertising. You may not have the funds in place for a large advertising campaign, but you can and should design advertising campaigns which reflect a certain percentage of your actual budget. Not including advertising in your budget is not an option.

For this exercise, you need to answer the question as if money were not an issue. Remember, when considering methods and procedures, money is not to be taken into consideration. Money is, of course, important, but this is not the place to scrimp. In chapter 9 we will explore marketing plans in a creative way in which we learn to put efficient marketing programs in place that do not require a lot of money.

Profitability is our next subject. Many agents think of it as a destination. They figure that when the year finishes, they either have the proper numbers and are in line to receive additional compensation, or they are not. That is a mistake. Profitability is not a destination; it is a journey. The decisions that you make every day, the procedures that your team follows every day, will determine if you get there or not. Of course you can't prevent a catastrophe in which your area gets hit with a major storm. If that happens, you will see profitability (i.e., bonuses) go down for the year. But your procedures and the training that you give your employees will determine in the long run your profitability index. The most important thing to remember is that profitability is not "luck"; it is a science and a result of your agency's daily business decisions.

It is crucial to your operation that you make sure your team sticks with the procedures you've put in place in order to maintain profitability. Also, it is important to remember to identify the type of customers you want to bring to your agency before adding the new prospect to your book of clients. By pre-underwriting, such as taking pictures of vehicles before adding full coverage to a policy, taking pictures of homes before binding coverage, etc., your agency should be profitable at the end of the year. In chapter 4 we will cover profitability in greater depth. What you need to decide now is your profitability goal. The higher the goal, the more you will have to filter your prospects before you add them to your agency as clients, and the more you will have to comply with your pre-underwriting procedures.

I just want to briefly have you start to consider your views and strategies for keeping your **retention** levels at their highest, since retention is a key factor in the insurance industry. In our business, the commission for one or two months is not enough to put food on the table and to run a successful business. In addition, the carrier or carriers that you represent may not reach a break-even point until the policy has been in force for a number of months. We must project a lifespan for our policies of at least ten years. In chapter 4 we will cover retention procedures in greater depth to help you achieve your goals. For now, you must give some serious thought to what those goals should be. Here I'd like you to ask yourself the percentage of clients that you are going to aim to have with more than just one line of business insured by you. What I mean is the percent-age of clients that are going to have **multiple policies** with your agency, such as an auto policy and a home or commercial policy, or life insurance with your agency. This percentage will directly impact your retention numbers. It is difficult to grow an agency with the majority of the clients insured in only one line and to keep good retention numbers. For the most part, cli-ents would prefer to have all their insurance policies under one agency. If you have been in this business for any length of time, you've seen firsthand that the clients who have mul-tiple policies with you are those that are stay-ing with you. If you've written only their auto or only their home they are more likely to eventu-ally move that single policy. If you are not the agency that is going to solicit all of their insur-ance needs, another agent will solicit them and you will lose the client altogether. A solid agency will have at least 80 percent of its clients covered under multiple policies.

Automation is another extremely important item to factor in. If you represent a direct writer, the company that you represent will provide you with its automated system. However, if you are in the independent world, you must decide on an agency management system that is user-friendly and offers adequate training and long-term customer service. I have discussed this with many independent agents who say that they don't have the funds to invest in a management system. If you don't start with professionally developed software that will help you manage your clients, you will not have the information that you need to maintain, upsell, and manage your customers. If you are serious about opening an insurance agency that is going to be known for its success and strength, consider investing in an agency management system from day one.

Moving right along, the next item that you must determine is the number of locations from which you will operate. Opening a separate location has many advantages, as well as challenges. This part may be easier in the independent world, but we'll cover this area more in depth later. Many captive companies may not allow an agent to operate from multiple locations.

You can visit www.TheInsuranceProfession. com and download the **Executive Vision document** from the Resources tab. It will be an instrumental tool for you to visualize your choices and map a path for your agency.

Now that you have had a chance to identify the DNA of your operation, write a document that contains the vision of the agency and all the components identified in the **Executive Vision document.** This way you can see it at a glance. You may want to share some of these areas with your employees so that they will know the direction of the company. Attempt to create a list of "Ten Commandments" for your agency and display them so that your team knows them by heart.

CHAPTER 3

Creating a Winning Team

I can't give you a formula for success, but I can give you a formula for failure: try to please everybody all the time.

HERBERT BAYARD SWOPE
American editor and journalist;
first recipient of the Pulitzer Prize

Now we are going on a quest to find out who you are as a manager. I am going to provoke you with some questions that you should ask yourself in order to help you discover your strengths and weaknesses. The first place to begin is to go back and remember every manager you have had since you were in high school and identify the qualities of the *best* manager you ever had. You admired that person for a reason. What we are looking for are adjectives that best describe what you saw in that manager— for example, a good trainer, always available when you had a question, patient, good leader, good communicator, clear in his or her direction. If you are able to identify the qualities that you admired in that manager, you will become more conscious in evaluating the differences between your current management style and the improvements you would like to make in order to achieve those qualities. We have the tendency to imitate that which we admire.

Now go back in time and try to remember the *worst* manager you ever had. It is important to do this exercise so that you can remember how it felt being managed by a person with those weaknesses—for example, the micromanager who was always looking over your shoulder, never trusting that you would do a good job; the manager who was critical of your work and never expressed to you that you did a good job; or one who was distant and insecure. Every manager has weaknesses and strengths. However, I can remember more managers with weak leadership skills than those I truly admired who were strong leaders and set a good example for their employees.

When it comes to management, the law of the farmer applies. What you sow, that you will also reap. As managers, sometimes we plant potatoes and expect carrots. For example, if you never trust that an employee will do a good job, you cannot expect that employee to take on and own a project for you. Your actions will be so critical of the ways and methods of every task that you delegate that, as a consequence, you will cause employees to fear disappointing you so much that they will never take ownership of that project.

Let's compare two scenarios. As the manager of your agency, you want your employee to contact policyholders whose policies are lapsing. You tell your employee that every morning, the first thing he will do is to go to the insurance company site, find the policies that are lapsing, and call those clients before 10 a.m. You tell your employee verbatim what to say when he calls. You want that to be done without fail, and you tell your employees that you will be paying attention that this gets done every day. On the surface, there is nothing wrong with this. Now, let's examine for a moment another approach. You sit down with your employee and you tell him that one of the cores of your agency is to make sure that every customer gets contacted when his policy enters a lapse stage. You tell your employee to come up with a plan, write down the process of how to accomplish this objective, and let you know those procedures by the end of the day. At the end of the day, the employee comes to you with a concise plan of where he will go to find the policies lapsing. He also tells you that it is best to contact the customer first thing in the morning, because once the day starts rolling, there will be many distractions and phone calls so that it will be hard to get this done later.

Let's compare both approaches. In the first one you communicated to your employees by your instructions that *you* are directly responsible for the success of the project and they are just the people executing your instructions. There is no personal reward for the employees when the project succeeds. Therefore, there is no ownership. In the second scenario, you communicate to your employees that they are the managers of the project and totally responsible for its success or failure. The biggest difference is that in the first scenario *you* own the project, and in the second scenario, *your employee* owns the project. You will still supervise it to make sure it gets done, but you don't own it. In this scenario, adding an extra incentive for a job well done may even get you more creativity from the employee to get the job done more efficiently. Also, it is very important in the second scenario that you give recognition to that employee, which will serve as inspiration to the team to follow this example.

Develop tools that help you manage, so that your employees are owners of their jobs and you merely the supervisor. While you have given ownership of a project to an employee, it remains your responsibility to ensure that the job gets done as agreed. Having a regularly scheduled check-in may be necessary for awhile until you're sure that what was promised is being achieved.

It is crucial that you train your employees never to damage your trust. If they own a project that you have delegated to them, *they* must make sure that it gets done. And when it cannot get done, for whatever reason, they need to communicate that to you. This may require some initial training and patience on your part. But the success is guaranteed. Many of my employees have come from environments in which they are told what to do and how to do it. When I share with them the concept of owning the project, they feel very insecure at first. If they never have owned a project, in the beginning they may stumble a few times and ask a lot of questions. They may even test you to see if you really mean what you say. If you find out that an employee is not doing what he has committed to do, you will communicate again that if he doesn't own the projects he has have committed to, he may not belong in your organization. During my management life, I have supervised over five hundred employees. I have never had an employee that didn't end up taking ownership or leaving my organization of his or her own accord. If people choose to be irresponsible, this type of atmosphere makes them very uncomfortable.

When employees succeed at owning their projects and achieving success, you *must* give them credit for it. Sometimes you may follow up with a reward. You must always acknowledge verbally that they did a good job and they have earned your trust. Micromanaging is not only an exhausting experience for you, but it diminishes your potential to grow. Most projects can be done in different ways and still achieve success. If you let your employees select the method to accomplish the task, they own it and your job is only to create the tool to supervise it.

Let's talk about finding a good employee. First of all, you must admit that there is no "perfect" employee. Remember that we are all different and there is no other person like you in the world, so make sure you're not wasting your time looking for someone just like you. You must evaluate your expectations and identify what your idea of a good employee is.

Let's put together a list of questions that you might discuss with someone you are interviewing:

1. Describe the job that you have enjoyed the most.

When the interviewee describes the best job, you are going to look for signs that will let you know if the candidate is an introverted or extroverted person. It is very important for you to know if the person you are interviewing fits the job description well. For example, the candidate may say he enjoys working in an office where the phone doesn't ring a lot (which indicates an introverted personality), or he may enjoy an environment in which there are lots of people around with the phone ringing and clients coming into the office (extroverted personality).

2. Describe the worst job that you ever had.

Question number two confirms your perception of the personality profile that you discovered in question number one.

3. What is it that you admired the most in your previous managers?

It is very important to know the qualities that an applicant admires the most. You want to obtain the highest productivity levels from your employees. If you know how to delegate assignments to your employees, you will know how to obtain the greatest production. During one of my last interviews with a candidate, she told me that she likes to work with projects and deadlines. She was also able to identify that she didn't work well under a micromanager who gets involved in every step of the process. She likes to own the project and get it done within the time frame allotted for completion. That is valuable information for me to know.

4. What did you dislike the most about your previous managers?

This question confirms your evaluation in question number three. It is important to corroborate your evaluation from a different angle to make sure that it is accurate.

5. If I contact your prior manager, what would he or she tell me about your attendance and punctuality?

Attendance is related to dependability. By asking this question you are not telling your candidates that you are going to call their prior employer, but it is worded in a way that they know they cannot hide the correct answer from you because you may call. It is not the same question as, "Were you on time and dependable at your last job?" What do you think they are going to tell you? If you ask "*If* I contact your prior employer…" the answer may be totally different.

6. Tell me about a situation in which you used your creativity to solve a problem at work.

This question attempts to give you an example of how your candidate can perform best. Remember that even though you pay an hourly wage, your employee agrees only to exchange his or her time for money. He or she is willing to also give you his or her commitment and creativity, but usually that is something you have to earn. These questions are designed to help you know how to earn it.

7. Other than money, what else is important to you in a job?

It isn't a fair assumption that all employees are mainly motivated by money. There are many things that motivate all of us that are not related to finances. They may tell you about their favorite restaurant, or perhaps they like to go with their family to the zoo or to play golf; perhaps what they like is going to the movies with their spouse. If you want to know what incentives to give your employees that would motivate them to work hard for your company, this question will help you find the answer.

8. Tell me about your hobbies. What do you enjoy doing in your spare time?

This question tells you if a person has learned how to enjoy life. Knowing what someone does to unwind is very important to you. As an example, someone that works hard for you and then goes home to take care of small children and the household chores without having discovered how to unwind may not be as happy, dependable, and healthy as you may prefer. Hopefully you will find that the candidate has found ways to avoid a buildup of stress while at home, which is very important in order for a person to perform his or her best at work.

After all the questions have been answered, it is time to share some of your basic expectations. You may start by saying that he or she has to get to work on time. You may continue by explaining that in your organization, you only have people that are creative in problem solving and independent thinkers that own their projects and achieve success without your moment-by-moment supervision. You can also explain that in your organization, your employees get rewarded in different ways when the job gets done well. If the person that you are interviewing is the type that just wants a job but has no intention of committing to your organization, this structure will make him very insecure. I have gone as far as explaining to the candidate that I am looking for the right person to complete our award-winning team. I gave the example that many people want to be a part of the Olympic team, but very few actually qualify. I then explain that the existing team has achieved a leadership position in the industry, and they are very passionate about what they do. I then ask, "Do you think you would like to be a part of this team?" What I just did is create a picture of the cohesive atmo-sphere and teamwork in the office. If this per-son is not willing to give her best and just wants to exchange time for money, she can imagine the pressure that will come from the other team members if she doesn't don't perform, and at the same time she can imagine how reward-ing it would be to be around competent people that work as a team and achieve high levels of success.

Let's go back to the beginning of the chapter and talk about you now. You have identified the qualities of the best manager that *you* ever had. I would be willing to bet that among those qualities, trust is near the top of your list. Your best manager was someone who trusted you, and you trusted him or her as well. Someone that was secure enough in who he or she was that he or she wasn't afraid to let you accomplish the job, make mistakes, and learn from them.

I frequently ask my employees for an evaluation of me as a manager. I ask them what it is that they like the most about my management style and what they would like to see me improve. We have created an environment that is based on trust. They have no problem letting me know if I do something they resent. If I want to obtain the maximum potential out of my employees, I have to pay attention to their comments. This exercise is essential to working as an efficient team. We are all equally important. The only difference between all of us is our functions within the organization.

The objective of every employer is to obtain the employees' maximum potential. In order to do this, you must know their strengths and weaknesses. A sense of accomplishment is a mandatory ingredient if we want to reach our maximum potential. I ask my employees which project or functions within their job description they enjoy the most. I realize that it is in doing the projects they enjoy the most that I see the most productivity. We all have to do some things throughout the day that we may not necessarily enjoy, but, as much as possible, I strive to divvy up the workload according to personalities that fit the task. Let me show this to you by way of an analogy. If a 4X4 were to race on a speedway, it would perform very poorly among the Formula One vehicles. It would feel that even though it is giving its best, the other cars pass it without any effort, and there is no chance of ever winning a race. However, if it races on a dirt road where the 4X4 shines, it wins medals and feels accomplished. Assign projects within your organization that match the areas of skill, accomplishment, and satisfaction of your employees. Good results will be inevitable.

There is a lot to cover in this arena. However, I must not finish this chapter without mentioning the most common and perhaps worst mistake of many managers. I have had quite a few managers who never told me I was doing a good job. Their philosophy was that there is always room for improvement. Out of insecurity, they feel that if they tell you that you did a good job, you will not give your best on the next project. The opposite is true. As an employee, my emotional reaction was that it didn't matter how hard I worked, I would never please my manager. Why should I work so hard the next time? What was the reward that I received for my best efforts? It is important to recognize that people are not computers in which, at the press of a button, the executable program kicks in and gets the job done. One of the most important components of human beings is their emotions. The best feeling that you can give an employee is a sense of accomplishment.

For every project, there must be a destination. If you want to increase sales, select a period of time—one month, for example—then set a specific, *reachable* number and put in check points along the way to ensure progress. If you want to increase retention, select the percentage which you would like your agency to reach, as well as a specific time frame. Make sure that you have the right tools to measure improvement. Explain where you are today and where you want to go in the time period selected. Get everyone focused on the goal and celebrate (I mean throw a party!) when those goals have been accomplished. Could they have done a better, more efficient job? There is always room for improvement. However, if your specific goal was accomplished, take the time to commend the employees that made it happen. Create achievable goals and ways to maintain your employees' focused efforts, and then celebrate their accomplishments when they get there! An atmosphere of hard work *and* celebration creates a healthy and fun environment.

Before you post a job opening in your organization, identify the projects or tasks that form the job description. This will help you identify the strengths that the candidates must have in order to achieve success and reach a sense of accomplishment. Going back to my metaphor, don't hire a 4x4 to race on a speedway. During the interview process, you must explain exactly what the job entails and the qualifications that a person must have in order to achieve success. If you hire an extroverted person who thrives on interaction with others to manage your filing system and customer records, that person will not be happy and will have difficulty achieving success.

Here I'll add a brief word of warning regarding hiring family members or close friends of your existing employees. There are some benefits but also some unforeseen pitfalls to doing so, and I'd suggest avoiding this if possible in the best interest of all concerned.

CHAPTER 4

The Three Cores

If you must play, decide on three things at the start: the rules of the game, the stakes, and the quitting time.

CHINESE PROVERB

The three pillars of our industry are *profit-ability*, *customer service*, and *retention*. If we miss even one of the three, we will not stay in this business for very long.

Before we cover the three cores of our business we need to lay some groundwork. It is very important that we know what we sell. Why is it that some people are not insured even though it is unlawful to drive without insurance? Why is it that some people have a hard time paying for their insurance? Why is it that some people walk into your agency and request the state minimums? Here is the answer: What we sell is an intangible item. People pay a lot of money for insurance but don't have a product to show their friends or family. It doesn't have an impact on the perception that society has of them. A large percentage of the population seems very concerned with what peers, friends, and family think of them. I have had people walk into my agency and request a quote for their newly purchased auto. When I told them how much it was, they told me that they spent all of their budget money on the car payment and had no more money to pay for the insurance policy that would help protect that asset. It was more important to them to stretch for a higher payment so they could show the world their status in the form of a car than to pay for the insurance policy to protect it. We sell intangible items; we solicit people to spend money, and in return they don't have anything to show for all that money. I think people may also feel that they spend a lot of money that they never get back if they don't need it – for example, they buy car insurance but never have an accident. You and I are aware of the importance of being properly covered, but most people are used to purchasing "things," not a piece of paper that tells them that they own something that they may or may not need someday. It is very important for us in the insurance sales business to understand the dichotomy that people experience when they purchase insurance from us.

Let's dig deeper into the three main objectives of your business.

The first and probably most important piece for *staying* in business is *profitability*. Many of us insurance agents don't quite understand this objective. In any other industry, if you make a sale, you have done your job. For example, let's examine the real estate industry. When the customers sign the papers for the purchase of their new home, the salesperson has done his job. He receives the commission, and after the sale, profitability is not an issue. The salesperson has contributed to the profitability of the company by the sale of the house. The salesperson's job ended with that sale. For those of us in the insurance sales industry, it is a lot more complicated than that. When we sell our first policy, our job for the client has really just begun. We need to make sure that we pre-underwrite the risk before binding coverage. We need to inspect a vehicle that needs full coverage and has had a lapse in coverage. We need to inspect a home before binding coverage to make sure that it is insurance worthy.

We as insurance agents are businesspeople who need to understand the term "being profitable" to stay in business. Or, to simplify, if your overhead is higher than your income, you will not stay in business for very long. The same is true with the insurance carriers that we represent. If we don't bring them good risks, they will not be able to stay in business for very long. Just like us, they are in the business of making money.

Before we go any further, let's define a "good risk." History, or legend, tells us that the insurance industry started in the old country of England when people in a bar would bet on a new ship making it all the way to the new world. Some people bet that it would sink and other people bet that it wouldn't sink. That is how insurance companies were formed. They collected money from the bets on the ships that didn't sink to have money to pay for the bets on the ships that did sink. That evolved into the ship owners paying a fee, or premium, betting that their ship would sink. The "insurance company," after inspecting the ship, cargo, and crew, would bet that the ship would not sink, and if it did they would pay the owner to purchase a new ship. If you think of it this way, an insurance policy is a bet. The policyholder bets that his house is going to burn and the insurance company bets that it is *not* going to burn.

In order for an insurance carrier to make money, we, the agents, need to make sure that the risks that we bring are worthy of an insurance policy. Going back to the old English legend, who would bet that a certain ship would make it to the new world if the ship was run down and in need of important repairs? You would not bet on a ship like that after you inspected it and saw its poor condition. It is the same with the insurance carriers. If you have the authority to bind coverage representing an insurance carrier, why don't you inspect the risks you "bet on" for the company? If you think that just by making the sale of a policy you have contributed to profitability, you are mistaken. Profitability comes after you have inspected the vehicle and have seen that the owner takes good care of it and has a good driving record. You "bet" on behalf of the insurance carrier that, given the good record of your client and the good condition of the vehicle, nothing is going to happen to that vehicle, and the policy is going to be claim-free for many years. That, in a nutshell, is how you maintain a profitable book of business.

I have to finish by saying that in my opinion, next to doctors, we have the highest privilege of any industry in the service community. When people are hurting the most because they have experienced a major loss in their lives, we, the insurance agents, get to deliver the money needed to help bring them back to where they were...with money that is not ours (the premiums of other insureds pay for the loss through the carrier). People will never forget how *you* helped them in their time of need. When people are experiencing hardship, their emotions are very involved, and it is a unique opportunity for you to make an impact on them. It is showtime for you. You have a chance to demonstrate to your clients why they selected you over the competition. Never let a claim opportunity pass you by. Make the most of it.

Here are a few tips that may help you increase your profitability:

- Very important: Always list *all* the drivers in a household. You may be shocked by how many vehicles you insure in your agency and the number of drivers *not* listed on the policies. When a client has an accident, always make sure that the driver involved in the accident is listed on the policy. If not, you need to start asking questions.

- If there has been a lapse in coverage, never insure a vehicle with a full coverage policy until you or your staff inspects the vehicle. If the car is not present when the client requests the policy, put liability only on the vehicle and ask him or her to drive it to your office for inspection.
- Never bind coverage on a home that you have not inspected. You may be surprised at the condition of some of the houses that are being purchased or refinanced whose owners come to your office requesting insurance. *Always* inspect the properties that you insure. If the property is far from you, make sure that the pictures you are seeing are current. I just heard of a new policy written on a motel based on the

pictures that the assessor's office provided. The pictures were very outdated. The motel building was so run down at the time of the application that part of the building's roof had collapsed. After the insured took the policy, he submitted a claim. He had the intention to have the insurance company pay for years of bad maintenance. Insurance carriers cannot run a profitable business in situations like this, and neither can you.

- When a client comes to your office to purchase insurance, have a list of questions that you ask of *everyone*, *every time*, to understand his or her needs. In medical terms, you must always remember that in order to prescribe, you must first diagnose. You may have the product that solves the client's problem, but make sure that you understand the problem first in order to sell the correct product.

These are just a few tips among many to help you retain your clients.

The next core of our business is *customer service*. Before we go any further, we must address the poor reputation that our industry has regarding customer service. What industry do you know of that has a customer for over ten years, paying a significant premium every single month, and when the customer needs to get in touch with his agent, the phone call goes to voice mail? What industry do you know of that has a customer for over fifteen years, paying a significant premium, and has never even met his insurance agent? I know many agents who let every phone call go directly into voice mail, and some that maintain no contact with their clients whatsoever.

The quality of customer service that other industries have achieved is due to the competition. If a customer calls a real estate agent to buy a house and the phone call goes to voice mail, the customer dials the next agent in the phone

> Price is the **number four** reason why people change insurance companies. **Lack of service is number one.**

book. Since many insurance agents don't even answer the phone when our customers call, our industry must not be afraid to lose them. You may say it is too expensive to hire people just to be able to answer every time the phone rings. And you may be right. However, can you afford not to be there for your customers when they call?

This example is just one of the many things our industry does to its customers that would not be permitted in other industries. We are going to see major changes in the sales and customer service part of the insurance industry in the near future. The consumers are getting smarter every day and demand excellent service. Remember that the consumer dictates the quality of customer service that he or she wants from you. Research shows that lack of service is the number one reason why people change insurance companies…price is number four. As an insurance agent, you can't afford not to deliver the best quality of customer service to the clients that are faithfully paying you a premium every single month. Insurance premiums are a good portion of an individual's or a family's budget. The consumer is demanding the same sacrifice from you in customer service quality. If we think that as agents we own the client, we are sadly mistaken. The clients decide to "park" their business at our doorstep until they find something better. Make sure to show your appreciation for their business on a regular basis, and create a culture in your office of excellent customer service.

In order to talk about *retention*, we need to understand that we sell a "small ticket item." It is very difficult to survive on first commissions from a new policy. If you believe that a sale is a sale is a sale, you are in the wrong industry. You could be making a lot more money if you were selling another product that has higher margins, such as a home or a mortgage or a car. The money in the insurance industry is in retention. During my years in this business I have met agents who have what is perceived as a large agency with many employees, but their profit margin is less than a small two-person operation, the difference being that the smaller agency has a retention of 90 percent or better. The agency that has very poor retention has to hire more employees to continually sell new policies because it cannot keep the policies that it already has, as well as keep reinstating the policies that lapse or cancel for lack of payment. The common mistake that agency owners make is to think that throwing more people at the problem will fix it.

In order to keep your retention level high, here are some suggestions to help your agency:

- Always suggest that clients use EFT as the payment method. If their money is tight, they will always pull from another source rather than cancel the scheduled EFT payment.

- Know your clients well. Make notations in your agency management system about your customers' hobbies, their children and family information, etc. This will help you *connect* with them. Connecting brings trust, and it is the best value that you can bring to your customers. It is also what gives you an advantage over companies that advertise on price alone.

- Upon every renewal, send customers a letter of gratitude for their business. The carrier may send them a letter as well, and that is good, but *you*, as their agent, must *also* send them a letter thanking them and offering your assistance in the event that they may need your expertise and service.

- Every week, run a list of all the clients in your book of business who are cancelling or lapsing. Make a phone call giving them an opportunity to make a payment over the phone. Many clients' policies are lapsing because they may be going through some difficult times and may have forgotten to pay the bill, or the bill got sent to the wrong address or got lost in the mail. As previously mentioned, you may come up with a program in your agency whereby you will call a customer up to three times in a twelve-consecutive-month period. You can inform the customer when he or she reaches the last warning phone call that if he or she lapses again, you will not be able to call. Your agency management system will assist you in tracking how many calls you have made due to lapsing. Once you put that program in place, you must adhere to it with no exceptions. If you have to call a client more than three times in a twelve-month period due to lapsing, you have to wonder if that is a client that belongs in your agency.

- Research shows that you can increase your retention by putting your name in front of your customer at least four times a year. Remember that your customer is being bombarded with ads from the competition on a daily basis between every renewal of the policy. If you don't keep in frequent touch with your clients, you may lose them to the competition.

- Another observation regarding retention is that people don't like change. It takes energy and time to shop for your insurance. It is very important for you to know why your customers invested their time and energy to leave your agency. Sometimes, it is our own system that kicks our customers out of our agency and right into the lap of the competition. For example, a homeowner's policy renews, and the insurance carrier sends the bill automatically to the mortgage company. Let's say that the mortgage loan has been sold to another financial institution and the bill gets returned. Therefore, it never gets paid. If you don't take the time to see who is renewing every month and who is lapsing, your system will be forcing some of your clients out of your agency.

- Always get in touch with clients when they have a claim situation. As I said, a claim is showtime for the insurance agent. If you help your customer in her time of need, you will be surprised how many referrals will come your way. If you don't provide the service, the client may leave you and/or speak poorly about you to many people. You cannot afford that.

- When a customer informs you that he wants to cancel his policy with your agency, attempt to obtain more information that may provide an opportunity to save the client, or will at least keep you from losing others in the future.

- Always send letters of gratitude to customers that cancel their policy with you for the time that they have been your customers. If they leave for a specific reason, thank them for their input and tell them that you are going to make sure the same situation doesn't happen again. Keep them in your database and continue to send them Christmas and birthday cards. You may be surprised with the number of people that leave your agency and then end up being dissatisfied with their new agent, or a direct company, and will end up bringing their business back to you. Never remove a client from your list unless he requests it.

- I strongly recommend that you do annual insurance reviews with your customers. When you spend the time listening to changes that your client has experienced in the last year, it may expose new assets that need protection and will make a big impact on their loyalty to you.
- Never let an opportunity go by to get all of the client's insurance business. Most importantly, make sure you offer a life insurance quote to everyone. The more policies you hold, the more clients you hold.

Again, there are many other strategies that you can use to increase your retention; I wanted to list at least a few for you here.

CHAPTER 5

Forming Your Team

Do your own thinking independently.
Be the chess player, not the chess piece.

RALPH CHARELL
Author

Create a flowchart to identify the positions that you need filled.

Before we start hiring people, we need to create a flowchart in order to identify what those people will be doing. Even though this may seem obvious, you would be surprised at how many insurance agencies don't have defined positions before they start filling them. I need to take just a little bit of time emphasizing how important this exercise is in order to run an efficient agency. To make my point, I'll use another automotive analogy. Let's imagine that we are building a car. If we don't plan ahead, we may buy two steering wheels and three carburetors because we find a good deal. Never mind that you only need one of each. In a way it is the same with people. Some people have the skills and personality to sell; others are better with customer service; still others may have a gift for administrative work. If you, as the agency owner, only hire *bodies*, you may find that you hired two *steering wheels* when you only needed one.

What is a flowchart? It is a simple exercise which can even be fun. You start by drawing a box at the top with the title "Agency Owner." Directly underneath it, you are going to create other boxes according to the vision of your agency and how big or small you want your business to become. You may have a box for "Customer Service"; another for "Producer"; and maybe one for "Account Manager." The smaller the agency, the more duties each person has to take on. If you have a vision to create a large agency, you can divide up the work in many different ways, but having a *chart* will not only help your employees take ownership of the items under their "box," it also truly helps maintain the *flow*. Refer to Appendix A to see the skeleton of a flowchart.

Now, we need to define the job description for every box. These job descriptions are just suggestions. Make the necessary modifications to accommodate your particular business model.

Agency Owner

- Is responsible for the agency's growth
  - o Sets up new production goals every year
  - o Manages retention
  - o Manages losses
- Designs, implements, and manages marketing programs
- Manages the agency to maximize bonuses
- Manages employee incentive programs
- Manages staff and HR issues
- Handles finances, pays the bills, negotiates leases
- Is directly involved in maintaining and increasing the VIP clients

- Establishes and nurtures the outside agency relationships with district managers and insurance carriers
- Builds and maintains the reputation of his agency in the industry

Producer
- Responsible for increasing sales:
  o Joins leads groups
  o Establishes referral programs with outside sources, such as mortgage brokers, real estate agents, accounting firms, etc.
  o Establishes referral programs for existing clients
  o Creates agency associations to increase the flow of new business

Personality traits and skills for this job
- People person
- Sales closer

- Self-motivated
- Outgoing
- Computer literate
- Excellent telephone skills
- Team player
- Is able to handle rejection

Account Manager

- The most senior account manager may be the second in command. When the agency owner is not available, the senior account manager will temporarily take the tasks of the agency manager.
- Assists the agency owner with human-resources issues.
- Assists the agency owner and the pro-ducer with information and quotes to facilitate the sale.
- Manages the agency's VIP list.
- Provides a monthly list of the customers whose policies renew next month for the

customer service representative (CSR) to follow up.

- Contacts the customers who are involved in a claim to provide assistance and minimize the impact of the claim.
- Performs annual insurance reviews, starting with the VIPs.
- Runs weekly lapse/cancellation reports to manage the retention of the agency for the CSR to follow up.
- Contacts the customers with cancelled policies to see what the agency could have done better to retain the business.
- Sends letters to all the cancelled policyholders, thanking the clients for their business and making the agency available to answer any questions.
- Sends an annual letter to all former clients to maintain the contact and continue to put the agency in front of the client.

Personality traits and skills for this job

- Enjoys working with people
- Good manager
- Loyal to the agency manager and the agency owner and committed to the goals of the agency
- Leadership skills with the ability to hire and fire
- Outgoing
- Methodical
- Good with procedures
- Computer literate
- Excellent telephone skills
- Team player

Customer Service Representative (CSR)

- Assists customers with requests pertaining to policy maintenance
- Provides certificates of insurance for the customers
- Receives payments

- Contacts the customers who are lapsing
- Sends Christmas cards, birthday cards, etc.
- Is responsible for making sure that the customer's information in the agency management system is correct
- Sets up appointments for the annual insurance review for the agency manager and the account manager
- Is responsible for the emergency contact database
  - Enters new information
  - Sends information to the emergency contacts

Personality traits and skills for this job
- Detail oriented
- Methodical
- Good with procedures
- Computer literate
- Excellent telephone skills
- Team player

Administration

- Sends a letter to all the customers renewing next month, thanking them for their business and making your agency available to answer any questions regarding the policy. The list of those policies is provided by the account manager.
- Assists the insurance carriers with audits by providing the necessary information.
- Opens and distributes mail.
- Responsible for the storage and maintenance of the client's files.
- Responsible for entering new sales information in the agency management system.
- Answers the phone.

Personality traits and skills for this job

- Detail oriented
- Methodical

- Good with procedures
- Computer literate
- Good telephone skills
- Team player

I have seen many agencies grow without the benefit of a flowchart. The agency owner is also the manager; he has one assistant who is licensed; and they both do sales and customer service. When they are both overworked, the agency owner looks for another person who is licensed and who will also do absolutely every-thing. I know it's ridiculous to think of a doctor's office running this way, but let's look at how our model would play out there. The doctor would hire interns and nurses, and they would all visit with the patients, prescribe the medicine, go back to the front desk, answer the phones, update the patient files, enter the notes in the computer records, send invoices to the insur-ance companies for payment, collect co-pays from the patients, etc. When you visit your doctor, is that the structure that you want to see? How expensive would it be to have people who are licensed as doctors answering the phones, collecting payments, and maintaining the customer's files? Not just that, I can assure you that it would be a difficult endeavor to find a doctor who enjoys visiting with patients who is also good at filing and entering information in a computer. Absurd, yes, but that is basically what I've seen happen with many agencies. They are not only expensive but very difficult to run, let alone grow. If you want to eventually own a large agency, you need to add people specialized in different areas who use their own individual skills to the maximum potential. That is the whole point of the flow chart, and why you must update it and stick to it each time you are looking to hire a new employee.

I was working for an organization many years ago in which the manager came across a personality test and decided to administer it to each of his employees. The test focused on personality traits, such as introvert or extrovert, perceptive or intuitive, etc. The results were shocking. The organization found that it had introverts (those who enjoy working with projects and things more than people) answering phones in reception areas and being the first point of contact for the customer. They also saw that they had extroverts (those who need personal interaction to maximize their potential) filing customer documents in the back storage room. When the organization put every employee in its right place, the results were amazing. It improved performance and employee morale. Analogy alert: In a mechanics world, if you use the wrong tool to remove a nut from a bolt, you will stress the tool to the point of breaking it, and you will destroy both the nut and the bolt in the process. Every person is unique, and to ignore that can be a fatal mistake. In order to maximize your employees' potential, you must use the interview process extensively so that they can be fulfilled and realize their potential to the benefit of all.

As you grow to become a large agency, don't be afraid to duplicate jobs under the same job description. Perhaps as you grow you will need two producers before you need two customer service reps. You may need two administrators before you increase the customer service staff, etc. In addition, it would be a good idea to hire producers that specialize in an area such as personal lines or commercial lines. This will minimize training and maximize expertise, which always translates to increased sales.

When it comes to managing people, there is a very important thing that we must remember: our goal is to get the most out of an employee. The two most important things we can obtain from an employee are things we don't pay for and that you, the employer, must earn: commitment and creativity. If you believe that when you pay an hourly wage to an employee, you can demand those things, you are mistaken. You must constantly be making investments in your employees to earn both. You must create a culture in which investments are happening on a regular basis. You can do so in many ways; for example, celebrating birthdays, ordering lunch for the office every once in a while, taking them individually to lunch. Show interest by asking about their families, their hobbies, and the things that are important to them. Then, when you want to reward an individual for going above and beyond your expectations, you can surprise the sports fan with a ticket to a ball game, or the newlywed with a gift card to a restaurant. What you are doing is making relatively small deposits into an account that will yield great dividends. You'll begin to see that employees are volunteering both their commitment and creativity by staying after hours to finish something important for a client, or finding a creative way to solve a problem that earns a client's commendation. Of course, a paycheck is a driving force for the person filling out the application, but it's the continued positive affirmations that keep them loyal in the long run. In addition to the occasional gift, I think it's also important to have known incentives in place that producers and customer service representatives can strive to attain.

Now you know what kind of people you're looking for and how to motivate them to stay, but I want to give you just a few more tips that I've learned along the way, starting with day one.

➢ **The working atmosphere**: The very first day on the job, your employee will meet and probably ask others what it's like to work in your agency. That is why it is important that your culture is strong and you have confidence in the answers they'll hear. Keep in mind that whether there is cohesiveness or strife, the new employee will notice it almost immediately.

➢ **The "boss"**: If your intention is that the new employee report directly to someone other than you, he will have interviewed with that person first and then you. Make sure when the new employee comes in to work that his supervisor is the one now training and letting him know what is expected of him. It is important that new employees understand the chain of command and that they begin to develop a bond with their supervisor.

➢ **Training your clients:** One of my VIP clients became verbally abusive with some of my employees. After I had a conversation with the client and the situation didn't change, I was forced to let the client go. That sent a very strong, positive message to my staff that I cared about them, and was also a way to thank them for their commitment to me.

> **Clearly communicate your expectations:** Put your expectations in writing so that everyone knows what they are. Train your other managers to do the same. When your employees work hard to meet your expectations, they need to know that you are pleased with their work.

> **A training system:** Encourage a culture of continuous training. Further invest in your employees by sending them to various industry-related classes. As they become better professionals, that will reflect in the quality of your operation. This will also become obvious to your clients.

> **Keeping the best employees:** If you can't pay an employee the industry average, you need to communicate that and come up with a plan to increase his monetary compensation as soon as it is

viable. An employee will be loyal to you even if the pay isn't up to par with the industry if you create a healthy and fun culture in your office, and if he knows you are doing the best you can to increase his compensation as soon as you can. I have not had many employees ask me for a raise, because I make it clear that I will compensate them fairly and reward commitment and creativity…and then I do. I have also shared with my employees when the agency received a bonus. If you have an employee asking for a raise every few months, you may have to conclude that he'll never be satisfied and let him move on.

It is said that employees are the best asset of any company. I am going to challenge that statement. Only *good* employees are the best asset of your agency. Let's define a few of the traits of a good employee:

- Dependability—on time and with good attendance
- Creativity when it comes to problem solving
- Commitment to the agency and its vision
- Team player

Make a list of these traits and share them with your candidates for a new position during the interview process. This will give them a good idea of what is expected of them if they become your employees.

CHAPTER 6

The Glue that Holds it Together

(Creating a Culture)

I not only use all the brains that
I have, but all that I can borrow.

WOODROW WILSON
28th President of the United States

The culture of your agency is very important, not only to the success of your business, but for the longevity of your clients and the cohesiveness of your team. This concept became very apparent to me while reading the book *Good to Great: Why Some Companies Make the Leap…and Others Don't*, by Jim Collins. In it, Collins talks about the strong cultures of companies like IBM and Nordstrom and how they are a key element to their success. He further elaborates that companies with strong cultures can make an employee bloom, and employees who don't agree with the culture end up leaving. The same thing happens with customers.

What is a "culture"? Merriam-Webster defines it as "the set of shared attitudes, values, goals, and practices that characterize an institution or organization." My definition of a culture is the profound understanding of who you are…and who you are *not*. It's the difference between a one-size-fits-all uniform and a tailor-made suit. When you know your culture, your employees and your customers feel secure in the identity of your agency.

The culture of our company emphasizes a strong team atmosphere. We have had producers that wanted the benefits of a team but didn't want to participate with the team. They have what I call an independent style. When those producers who were interested in becoming a part of our company noticed the team atmosphere, they immediately knew they could not succeed in our culture. I recognize that there is nothing wrong with that. We want people who are comfortable working with the team and who will bloom in our culture. I have learned to explain our culture during the interview process to ensure there are no misunderstandings of who we are.

Create a team culture that is cohesive and is based on the "carrot approach" as opposed to the "stick approach." What I mean is that if you want your employees to do something, create an incentive that entices *them* to want to do it, as opposed to an order that must be followed. If, for example, you are having issues with tardiness, you could create an incentive whereby consistent punctuality is directly tied to a reward, as opposed to threats of punishment for further infractions. Fear of punishment is never conducive to creativity and performance. You want to establish a positive atmosphere in your office in which your employees are creatively solving problems and helping your clients. I highly advise a strong incentive program in your agency. Create an incentive for sales goals achieved for the salespeople; reward the account managers for retention; share a portion of your profit bonus with your employees so that they can be as motivated as you are in the running of a profitable operation. My employees know that there is a culture of rewarding extra effort, and, as I've previously mentioned, those rewards are not always monetary. Find incentives that may not cost very much but are of great value to your employees. I have found that gift cards are always a great motivator, but I never allow them to choose gift cards to places where they can buy essentials for their families. They can only select cards to special stores or restaurants that they may not be able to afford on a regular basis. They aren't the only ones who benefit from the reward either, because not only do they thank me with continued hard work, they often show off their purchases or tell me about the great time that they had while using the card. Another great gift is an overnight for two to somewhere special, yet local. I'm constantly amazed at the amount of motivational power brought on by an incentive that creates memories for an employee and the spouse, and once you get the spouse on board, you've gained an extra cheerleader in motivating your employee to keep up the good work.

I'll take a moment to share a particular success I had based on a culture of rewarding excellence. For a number of years I was the manager of a call center managing 225 people. The job itself was difficult for the employees; they were tied all day to a three-foot phone cord with calls coming in one after the other all day long. The monetary compensation was not enough to keep people motivated enough to continuously do a good job, or even to come to work every day. The culture in the center was to always be "coaching" those who were tardy, absent, had a poor job performance, etc. The manager's job was to spend all day coaching the poor performers. Furthermore, just as I was made manager, the client that this center was servicing gave the company an ultimatum that unless the performance of the employees improved, they would cancel the contract. The client gave the company six months to improve. As soon as I took the job, I changed the dynamic. I had less than ninety days to make drastic changes noticeable to the client. The first thing I did was to pay little attention to those that were doing a poor job. I still had to meet with them, but it was always a short meeting. I shifted all my attention to the good performers. I implemented incentives and healthy competition. I divided the group into twelve teams. The competition was to surpass the other teams in sales every week. I installed large whiteboards all over the area in front of each team so that everyone could see the improvements and how his or her team was doing. The winning team received awards and recognition. You'll be impressed at the positive impact a little healthy competition can bring to your team members and your agency as a whole.

I'll go further by telling you about a mistake I once made in the name of enforcing a strong culture. Some years ago I had created a strong and competitive sales atmosphere. Everyone was very focused on selling and we were constantly exceeding our sales goals. The result was that everyone was so focused on selling that no one was paying attention to retention. That was my mistake, and it cost our agency quite a bit of money. Our team was not worried about the quality of clients that they were bringing to the agency. Their only concern was to sell. There were several solutions to this problem. As soon as I realized where our agency was going wrong, I changed the strategy. Each week we gathered to monitor all the clients that were leaving us and all the policies that were lapsing. I changed the monthly incentive to reflect not only new sales but also the dollars we lost as a result of clients leaving us. Immediately I changed the target to consist of new sales minus dollars lost due to the clients leaving our agency. This was very effective. Every week when the team got together to evaluate the agency's sales against the goal, we also reviewed the names of all the clients that had cancelled that past week and the policies that were lapsing. It was amazing to me how the whole team got together to split the retention workload and split the names of the people canceling and policies lapsing to call them and to do whatever was possible to get them back to our agency. They were just as excited about that as they were about the new sales.

I encourage you to create a culture of rewards, awards, and recognition toward your employees to foster a fun and positive atmosphere. Just remember to monitor and adjust when necessary.

You also need to establish a culture for your clients, but first let me distinguish the three types of clients that you will have in your agency.

Average Client
  ➢ One line (auto or home only)
  ➢ Liability only (if auto)

- Minimum coverages
- Doesn't care about your presentation on coverages and exposure with lower limits
- Wants to make cash payments
- Lets his policy lapse frequently
- Price focused

Good Client

- Multiline (auto, home, boat, umbrella, life insurance, etc.)
- Understands the importance of having the appropriate liability coverage limits
- Wants to pay for his policies using EFT or pays in full
- Understands and values the relationship with his or her agent
- Price is not the primary focus when selecting his or her agent
- Refers people to you

VIP Client
- ➤ Has every quality of the good client
- ➤ High-dollar premium
- ➤ A pillar in your agency
- ➤ Strong relationship with the agent

Now that we have identified the three types of clients, let's translate that to our culture. Let's say that you have a culture that nurtures **good clients** and **VIP clients**. Knowing your agency's culture helps when you purchase an Internet lead that is looking for auto insurance, liability only, with lower limits. When you call him, he tells you he'll be paying cash and rebuffs your suggestions to meet in person to discuss his coverages. Knowing that there is a chance that this average client may become a good client in the future, you want to treat him with respect and meet his needs, but you also know that he doesn't currently fit in with the agency you are cultivating and probably won't stay long. The goal we strive to maintain is a client base of 80 percent in the good to VIP range and 20 percent average, so that's the amount of time and effort we're willing to expend in each range as well. Having that culture in place keeps us from spending an inappropriate percentage of our time on the clients that don't fit our model. We don't want to spend more than 20 percent of our time chasing lapses and cancellations, but we do want to spend that time trying to make inroads and develop a relationship so that once that client gets more established in his career and family and starts seeing the benefits of covering his accruing assets, we'll be there.

There is one important fact we need to understand. Currently most of those people wanting insurance with liability only and with minimum coverages may tend to shop for, and purchase, their insurance via the Internet. The two leading Internet insurance companies, Progressive Direct and Geico, have figured out how to make money with what we call average clients, and that's who they market to. Those companies have identified and communicated their strong culture based only on price. We see that by their advertisements, because the emphasis in the ad is how much the average customer saves by switching to them. You *cannot* and *should not* compete with their culture. In these commercials there is no mention of anything other than savings that they bring to the table, and for a certain demographic that's all it takes. Make sure that when you advertise your agency, you mention your culture and what your clients value the most. That is what I call your value Proposition. You should post your value proposition prominently in your agency so that your employees and clients can see it. Explain, emphasize, and celebrate your culture. It will bring you success, profits, and stability.

CHAPTER 7

Managing Your Time

What gets measured gets managed.

PETER DRUCKER,
Management theorist, author of thirty-one books,
recipient of the Presidential Medal of Freedom

You are at the center of the hub; the leader of your business. People depend on you and your energy to continue to perform at the highest level. The question is, how do you become more efficient?

Many people believe that the way to become more efficient is to cram more things into an already full schedule. The consequence is that you end up extending your working hours until your day is totally consumed by your business. When you get to that point, you start working weekends. I titled this chapter "Managing Your Time" to get your attention, but the title is a misleading approach to effectiveness.

I have a theory that people do not need you consumed with busywork so that they can perform better for you. Your staff and clients need your ENERGY. If you think about it, it is not very pleasant to be around busy people. You prefer to be around people who are happy and excited about who they are and what they are doing.

Remember, people like to be around happy people. Happiness is contagious! Busyness is not!

A long time ago I interviewed for a job. During the interview process I asked the would-be boss, "Can you please tell me the things that you admire the most about *your* manager?" I knew that whatever she admired about her manager, those were going to be the same things that she would expect of me as a manager. She told me that what she admired the most about her manager was that he was available twenty-four hours a day. She could call him day and night, seven days a week, and he would answer his phone and come to the office on a minute's notice. Immediately I knew that the job was not for me. The way this person defined efficiency was by the amount of time devoted to the job. If you have to turn your life off so that you can be someone at work, you may be missing the boat of happiness.

Now, after saying that, I have to add that there are a few people I know whose job is more of a hobby to them and yet they spend a lot of time at work, not because they need to prove something or because they don't have a good home life, but because it is so much fun that they cannot stay away from it, like a child at play gets so excited that he doesn't even take time to eat. To these people, work equals happiness, and while it's fine for some, most of us have families and outside interests that require time and energy as well.

I considered titling this chapter, "Manage Your Energy, Not Your Time," which is precisely what I strive to achieve. How do you manage your energy? Let's go back to a racing analogy. Imagine we are all race cars (okay, so I'm a fan of the Disney movie *Cars*). Some of us are Rally race cars; some of us are Formula One race cars. What happens when you take a

Formula One car and put it on a dirt track next to Rally cars? The Formula One car spends a lot of energy, is frustrated because no matter how much energy he spends on the track everybody passes him, and he feels like he cannot go anywhere in life, because the only race track he knows is a dirt track. Now someone discovers his potential and places the Formula One car in the Indy 500. What happens? All his energy is applied to the track, and with half the effort he gains speed. Then he discovers that if he applies more energy, he is moving faster and faster. The energy applied to the wheels turns into speed. He doesn't slide around. His energy is managed and focused on the direction of the track. (I can't help but add a side note here. Many of us feel tempted to make that mistake with our children. Because we may have found the race track where we excel, we try to put our kids on the same track, and that's not always a good fit.),

There are many race tracks in our industry: sales, management, strategy, public relations, customer service, etc. You may also find that you enjoy personal lines better than commercial lines and financial services, etc. As the owner of your business, you need to find your track so that every ounce of energy that you apply into the business translates into speed. That is how you are going to win medals and become a leader. If you find yourself being bogged down, or burning out, check yourself to make sure you're still on the right track. Look through the list below and become familiar with the things that give you energy and the things that drain it away.

- While performing tasks that give you energy:
  - You feel fulfilled as you work
  - There is a high level of satisfaction when the task is done
  - Time goes by very quickly

- o You can't wait until you get to do it again
- ➤ Performing tasks that drain your energy:
  - o You wait until the last minute to do them
  - o You cannot take them off your mind when you are off work, dreading the moment that you have to do them
  - o You feel like you need a vacation right after you do them

We are all born with an energy battery built into our emotional system. It is just like the one in your car. When you start your car on a bright, sunny day, the engine runs the alternator that produces more electricity than the car needs to operate and sends it to the battery, where it is stored. On a rainy night, your alternator cannot generate enough electricity to run the lights and the wipers, so it takes the energy from the stored electricity in the battery.

Your emotional system operates in much the same way; doing the things that you enjoy creates an internal energy that gets stored in the emotional battery. Everyone around you can tell when you are charged up because you are happy and performing at high levels. By the same token, when you do things that you dislike, you take energy from the emotional battery, and it shows in your countenance and in your performance. If you have enough energy stored, you may be able to take on some of the things that drain you, but not for long periods of time. However, if you don't have enough stored energy to pull from, everyone around you will know it because you will be upset and short tempered.

The sad part of the story is that many of us live our lives demanding energy from a depleted battery. The consequences are unhappiness, stress, etc., that may lead to physical symptoms or more serious problems like ulcers, heart attacks, high blood pressure, and worse. I'm sure that as you read this, you can picture people you know who are running on empty as opposed to those who enjoy their lives because they are fully charged.

Find the things that charge your battery, at work and outside of work. A full battery is what I consider to be the definition of happiness. Tell your family, your friends, and the people that work for you those things that charge your battery and the things that deplete your emotional battery. You will be surprised how much they will support you. Everyone wants to be around happy and fulfilled people.

Once you have shared these things with the people in your life, find out the same information from your spouse, friends, and staff. Have them go through the same exercise of identifying the things that they like and dislike doing so you can help them attain a greater share of happiness for themselves. We did this exercise in our office not long ago. I was surprised at the number of things I was asking some of my staff to do that were draining their batteries. I also learned that some of my employees enjoyed doing the things that others hated. So we tweaked the flowchart and changed tasks according to the "battery meter" (remember, the flowchart is to be used for the common good and should be reevaluated as needed). Now people are much happier than they were before. From a time-management standpoint it's clear that when you are doing those things you enjoy, you are going to be much more productive. We have added more fun to our environment and people are happier, and once again we see that translated into satisfied customers and profitability.

From a manager's perspective, in order to maximize your ability to keep your battery fully charged, you'll want to hire people that complement you, not only on a skill level, but on an energy level. For instance, I have discovered that reading and answering e-mails depletes my battery in a very short period of time, and, probably just like you, I get a lot of them! I have a great assistant that is very patient and takes the time to read through my e-mail and bring to my attention only those that require action and those that I need to answer personally. The majority of them don't fit into either category, and I don't want to waste valuable time or energy weeding through them all. I have also communicated with all the business associates in our company that if they need something from me, the best way to reach me is to call my cell phone. I do my best to return all my calls promptly. I've surrounded myself with people who are similar enough to me to embrace our culture, and yet are different enough to take on the draining tasks that actually charge them up.

Summarizing this chapter:

➤ Identify what charges your battery and what depletes it.

➤ Communicate with others those results.

➤ When you hire staff, hire people that have the skills and enjoy doing the things that deplete your energy.

➤ Have your staff go through the same exercise and communicate with you and with each other what charges and depletes their batteries. You may be able to switch tasks to improve the office efficiency.

➤ Efficiency is directly tied to energy.

➤ Doing *more things* that you hate doing will not make you more efficient, even if you manage your time perfectly.

As you continue to grow, create a culture where it is okay for people to talk about tasks that deplete their energy. That doesn't mean that everyone is always going to do only what they like and nothing else, but the ratio needs to be healthy.

Good luck with this exercise. Put yourself and your staff on the right race track and win medals. Life will be fun!

CHAPTER 8

Administration

We create stress for ourselves because you feel like you have to do it. You have to. I don't feel that anymore.

OPRAH WINFREY
Actress and talk-show host

For salespeople, administration is one of the most boring things that we need to do to stay in business. We just want to go and make money by selling policies. The way we look at it, administrative duties do not bring us money. However, without strong administrative practices, your business will be weak and vulnerable to failure. Administration does many important things for your business and your clients, most importantly setting up practices and systems by which you protect both.

My wife, Lissa, has an incredible gift for creating and implementing effective administrative procedures. The information and procedures that I am going to share with you in this chapter are among the many things I have learned from her. She constantly strives to improve and streamline the way we operate, which in the long run not only saves us money, but keeps us compliant with errors-and-omissions (E&O) standards and out of harm's way.

I am going to start by focusing on practices that you may have in your office that expose your business to an E&O claim. As much as you may hate it, one of the most important things you need to implement is regular in-house audits. As you continue to grow, you cannot and should not supervise every single application that your agency writes. However, clean applications, signatures, proof of prior insurance, pictures of properties, etc., will protect your business from a dreaded errors-and-omissions claim. I would venture to say that other than doing something illegal, E&O claims are the single biggest threat to your practice. People lose their agencies when their current carrier cancels their E&O policy and they cannot find another company that will offer them coverage.

I want to share with you some of the other administrative practices that we have found to help us stay on track:

➢ Have someone in your office be responsible for looking over every application to ensure that the proper documents are there—copies of proof of insurance, car registrations, etc., but, most importantly, *signatures*. If you have a signature on an application, it would be difficult for a client to have a court award him compensation, or coverage for a certain claim, by saying that he didn't know what he was signing. Signoff sheets on lower or important coverages make the client more aware of their selection of coverage while adding another layer of protection for the agent in the event of a lawsuit.

➢ It is common knowledge that most E&O claims are not due to an agent's error, but from those of his assistants. You, as agent, go through all the licensing training, company trainings, insurance publications, etc., but your assistants may not. They may lack the knowledge to pro-tect your business from certain practices that expose you to an E&O claim. The best way to have your staff up to date is to have a culture of ongoing training in your office. You should have regular staff meetings, preferably on a weekly basis. This is when you discuss things like how to minimize an E&O claim, how to docu-ment conversations with your clients, and the importance of keeping all paper-work and signatures related to a sale on file and up to date. When available, send your staff to outside trainings to improve their skills.

➢ Have a double-check system in which two people are involved in looking at the documents before they are sent to a pro-vider or filed away. It is a good practice to have the salesperson who collects the documents and signatures hand them off to an administrative assistant person to look them over before sending off or filing away. If you fill out a certificate of liability for a commercial policy, have your assistant send that to the provider after making sure that the coverages listed are correct and up to date *before* sending it. If the insured requests a copy of the certificate of liability, stamp the certificate with the message "For information purposes only."

Another item that we should cover while we talk about administration is the idea of "going paperless." Some carriers offer to e-mail the policies to the clients in an effort to cut costs and save the environment. If the carriers that you represent have not gone paperless, you must scan every application and important document into the client's file and save it in your agency management system or on your server. Not long ago, we needed to regularly back up our server and store the copy outside of the office; now there is online backup support available which easily pays for itself in saved time and peace of mind. If your office is vandalized or involved in a fire, you will not lose the important information of your business even if you lose all of your paper files.

Another important administrative practice is to identify potential problems, then create procedures to avoid them or at least minimize their impact. Taking the time to put together a manual, including all the procedures that will get the job done effectively and consistently, will not only save you time in the long run, it will save you many headaches as well as protect you from E&O exposure.

CHAPTER 9

Marketing and Branding

The reasonable man adapts himself to the world;
the unreasonable one persists in trying to adapt the
world to himself. Therefore all progress depends
on the unreasonable man.

GEORGE BERNARD SHAW
Maxims for Revolutionists

I would like to share with you something very important that I learned in one of the classes I took toward my MBA in marketing. When you try to market a product, you must understand the three phases of the marketing process: the **attributes**, the **functional and psychosocial consequences**, and the **value**. In order to give you an example, we'll use an advertising campaign for a luxury car. Picture an expensive convertible being driven by a woman with long, flowing hair as the car hugs the road along a pristine coastline. The **attributes** describe what the product is, in this case a luxury automobile that has four wheels, runs on a combustion engine, has an automatic transmission, and takes you from point A to point B. Even though this *is* a luxury car, there are many products on the market that are luxurious vehicles. A compact car has essentially the same *attributes*, and I as a buyer may not see the point of paying the difference between the two products. Now let's examine the **functional and psychoso-cial consequences** of this product, which, as the name implies, have to do with the differ-ence between this product and the competition from a functional and a psychosocial stand-point. The luxury car is a more reliable vehicle with better-quality parts; it is safer and has an acceleration of 0 to 60 mph in thirty seconds. The psychosocial consequences have to do with status. When you drive a luxury car, you know that people around you notice the make (brand recognition), and that, along with supe-rior performance, gives you more confidence. Last, but far from least, is the **value**. *Value* is the main reason people purchase a product. It has to do with the emotions of the consumer. The real image portrayed in the ad for the lux-ury vehicle is the sense of freedom and inde-pendence that the woman *feels* when driving the convertible next to the ocean, the way she *feels* when other drivers look at her as though they wished they were her, the sense of power when she *feels* the acceleration. Then, the writing at the bottom of the ad drives the emotional message to the heart: **"you *deserve* this."** Notice that the appeal of this advertisement is not focused on the four wheels, nor on the fact that it can take you from point A to point B very quickly and reliably, and not even the fact that it may be economical to operate. It appeals to the emotions and how you'll *feel* while driving this vehicle. Buyers will pay much more for a product that holds a high emotional value for them.

Now let's translate this lesson to the insurance world. The attributes of an automobile insurance policy are that the company will pay to get your car fixed in the case of an accident, which can be very costly. The functional consequences have to do with the fact that the insurance company has contracts with very good repair shops that would guarantee the work as long as you own the vehicle. You may also have functions built into the policy, such as diminishing deductibles that reduce the deductible amount every year that you don't submit a claim. Another functional consequence may be that if you have an accident, the insurance company will send an adjuster to the accident and cut you a check for the repairs on the spot so that you can get your vehicle fixed right away. All of these functional consequences are what makes auto insurance policies different from one another.

In the insurance industry we tend to stop here at the functional consequence level. When you see an insurance company advertising on TV, the main message it portrays to the viewer is how fast it pays its claims. The commercial may show two cars involved in an accident, and the driver that has that particular insurance carrier gets a check for the damages right way.

"Mr. Insurance Company, let me share something with you: as a customer I will expect that you are going to take care of fixing my car right away. That is why I pay my premium on time every month." All the insurance companies must do that to stay in business. That is not going to make me want to purchase a policy from one insurance carrier over another, providing that both companies are reputable and A-rated.

We need to have a strong **value** message in order to make people want to purchase an insurance policy from us. If your insurance carrier is USAA, you are with it not only because of the attributes or the consequences; you are there because it is status to you. You may have been in the military forces, and that is a qualification for being able to purchase insurance from USAA. You perceive that as status. Price (which is an attribute) will not make you change to other insurance carrier. Your USAA policy reminds you of the adventures that you had while in the military and the tight connections with your peers. You may even pay more for that policy because it makes you *feel* nostalgic and patriotic.

Pay attention; this may be the most important advice that anyone will give you regarding marketing, and it has to do not only with obtaining new customers but also keeping your existing customers. As an agent you *must* know what your value is to your customers and be very effective in communicating and demonstrating it to them. You need to develop a value proposition, memorize it, put it in writing, display it, and live it. If you fail to do that, your customers will shop their policy with other agents or carriers, and you may lose them. Auto policies renew every six to twelve months depending on the insurance carrier. During the time between renewals, your customer is being bombarded by insurance carriers via radio, TV, billboards, and bulk mail to switch their insurance provider. Powerful advertising can be very convincing, and if your customer doesn't know your value proposition (or value the emotional connection he has with you), he could easily end up switching. You need to be contacting your customer several times every year, developing a relationship, and making an emotional connection; then, when he is tempted by the latest cartoon character offering a better price, he'll think of you and all the reasons he wants to stay put.

Here is the marketing part: when you know and communicate your value proposition effectively, your customers will stay with you and refer your agency to their friends and family. As we all know, there is nothing better than referrals. If they come to you because they understand your value proposition, it will be easier for you or your staff to close the sale and retain your new clients.

In order to illustrate another important principle, allow me another (nonautomotive) analogy that in my opinion is directly related to marketing. Marketing is like fishing. Every river and lake requires different lures to catch the indigenous fish. When I go fishing somewhere for the first time, I find myself asking the locals which lures work best, because I don't want to take the time to try every lure possible until I find the one that works. Don't you wish it was that easy when it comes to marketing? When I started representing a direct writer company, I was trying to figure out this industry, and in order to find what marketing strategies worked, I went around asking more experienced agents what worked for them. A good friend of mine, Cory Louthan, who at the time was an agent with the same direct writer, told me that in this industry you have to use multiple methods (or lures) to attract your customers. And he was right! Yet the question still remained: *what lures do I use?*

Like fishing, marketing is a science and an art. Once you know which lures to use, you can control your results. As agents, we all "fish in different ponds." You may target clients with a particular demographic, a particular age group, gender or lifestyle, or common interests, associations, etc. Your marketing strategy most likely will not work for everyone else.

It is very important to have a concise marketing plan that you can follow. You must list your specific advertising strategies, along with your expected results. Here is an example template that you can use to list your advertising strategies.

PROMOTIONAL MIX STRATEGY		
Advertising Components	**Date and Duration**	**Intentions**
Direct Mail Current Client	Four times a year	Solicit other lines we don't insure
Internet Leads	Monthly	54% of all households initiate their insurance shopping experience over the Internet
Referral Program	Twice a year	Use the current book of business to reach family and friends
Hand Out 50 Business Cards	Weekly	Reach other prospects among people with whom I cross paths regularly
Leads Group Membership	Weekly	Reach other prospects from people within the leads group circle
Public Relations		
Involvement in a Local Community Program	Monthly	Meet other people outside my regular circle of influence

Let's examine this chart. List the advertising components, the date and duration of the program, the yearly cost so that you can budget your marketing expenses, and your expected results. Create in your agency management system a tracking mechanism for every advertising component so that you can track where your business comes from. At the end of every quarter, you must evaluate your expected results with the actual results to see how your marketing strategy worked. That way you will be multiplying or removing "lures from your tackle box." If you follow this plan, at the end of the first year you will be able to accurately see the results you obtained from every advertising strategy and the cost associated with it. Let's say that you obtained 310 policies from mailing your existing customers asking for referrals four times a year. With that scenario you can calculate that every new policy cost your agency $5.67. Apply the same situation to the newspaper ad in the local paper. This year it brought you 400 new policies; therefore, the cost is $4 per policy. Since you ran this ad four times last year, your new strategy for next year is to run the ad twelve times, which should bring you four times as many policies.

Once you find what works for you, you will have the ability to know how much your agency will grow each year based on your own marketing strategy and the costs associated with it. You should discard the programs that don't work for you and increase the programs that do work for you, fine-tuning them to bring in even better results. This process takes some discipline from you and your staff, especially in the first year, since you have to ask every new prospect how he heard about you, but it is imperative that you do that if you want to learn the marketing formula that works for your agency.

CHAPTER 10

Build and Manage Your Agency

Life is too short to be small.

BENJAMIN DISRAELI

British Prime Minister

Earlier we discussed the importance of building an adequate foundation before you begin to grow your agency. It is imperative to know how big you want to grow, and where you want to go, before you even begin to build.

Once you've laid the proper foundation and are ready to build on it, there is a principle that you need to keep in mind. Your philosophy must match your procedures, which at the same time will translate to results. I highly recommend you seek out the booklet "Procedures Must Match Philosophy," by Lloyd Daigle. Below I'll share some of the takeaways I gleaned from that little book.

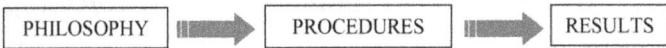

PHILOSOPHY	⟹	PROCEDURES	⟹	RESULTS

Let me illustrate this for you. Let's say that as a parent, you don't want your son to smoke when he grows older. This is the **result** box. Your philosophy is to have a talk with him when he is young so that he will understand the importance of not smoking and how bad it is for him. This is the **philosophy** box. The key is in the procedure. You are a smoker and your son has seen you smoking all of his life. Do you think that your son sees a connection between your **philosophy** and your desired **result**? Probably not!

Now let's apply this to your agency. As an example, your desired **result** is to have high retention in the agency. Your **philosophy** is that your employees will work hard at maintaining existing clients. If you don't create specific procedures for employees to follow and incentives for applying your procedures, your employees may not see a connection between your philosophy and your desired results. A good procedure may be to offer an incentive to every employee who convinces a customer to enroll in the electronic funds transfer program to pay his monthly premium.

Your function as a manager is to put the **procedures** in place that back up your **philosophy** to obtain your desired **results**.

I would like to show you how this will translate into profitability. Using your agency management system, print out a list of all your clients, then sort it by premium. That way you can identify your VIP clients, your good clients, and your average clients. Ask your staff to keep a log for one month of the names of the clients that they service. You may find that 80 percent of the clients calling your agency asking for service are on your average-clients list, representing only 20 percent of your book (lowest premiums, monoline, cash only). You may find that the clients that bring fewer premiums to your agency are costing you the most in staff hours. Let's evaluate the implications. As you continue to grow your book, you have to continue to hire staff to service your average clients. If your staff continues to spend time with the average clients, they have less time to make proactive calls to your good and VIP clients, to monitor and assist your clients with claims, to monitor renewals, etc. If your average clients are getting most of the attention of your agency, you are at risk of losing your good and VIP clients while the average customers continue to "reproduce." You should run this report every few months to ensure that you are spending your time and efforts servicing your VIP clients and good clients, who are not so demanding of your staff's time with much more lucrative **results**. If you are spending 80 percent of your time striving to satisfy your average clients, you'll find that they are referring your agency to other average prospects, and your VIPs and good clients not only are *not* referring good prospects to you, but your **procedures** may be causing them to shop for their insurance where there is an agent who will better appreciate their business.

Let's take a closer look at some of the pillars you have to create in order to build a strong agency:

MARKETING

Remember that marketing is a science. Once you find what works for you, you can control your production. You can make business decisions that will bring the correct number of producers to obtain the number of new customers you will acquire just by increasing the marketing efforts proportionally according to your expected results.

RETENTION

We sell what is called a small-ticket item. We depend on residual income to build our financial strength. For example, if you make $300 in commission for insuring a home and an auto, and you spend one hour to make the sale, if that client stays with you for ten years, you made $3,000 that hour. In order for you to make that money, you have to keep that customer for ten years. Agents that have low retention make less money per hour than those who have a good retention rate. Do the math and figure out what would happen to your yearly income if you were to implement a program that would add only 5 percent more to your existing retention. You will be amazed!

Excellence in customer service is at the heart of retention. Your customers refer your business to friends and family, explaining to them the positive experience of being your customer.

The essence of excellence is embedded in two things: relationships and giving back.

Developing close relationships with your clients is not an easy thing. It requires commitment from you and your staff. There are several ways to accomplish this. Here are some ideas to promote excellence:

Using your agency management system, use the notes section to record personal things about your client. I use it to record kids' names, anniversaries, hobbies, areas of interest. Your clients love to talk about these things. You can obtain that information in a simple conversation. Let's say that they tell you they love to fish and own a cabin next to a river. If they volunteer that information, it's because it is important. When your client calls you, as soon as he tells you his name, you need to pull up your notes so that you can be reminded while you're talking. During the business conversation, you should ask him what he pulled out of the river on his last trip to the cabin. This creates a deeper bond with your clients and makes it less risky when you need to call him to tell him that his rates have increased. Clients have an emotional bank account. As a matter of fact, we all do. If we find ways to make continuous deposits into the client's emotional bank account, we'll be okay when we need to make an occasional withdrawal.

Giving back to your clients simply means show them that you value them in tangible ways. During your conversations, make sure to discover what is important to them; listen for what excites them or puts a sparkle in their eye. Some clients may value praise; others, small gifts; and still others appreciate birthday cards for their grandchildren. These types of investments can make huge deposits in your client's emotional bank account. If you are like me, when I get a magnet from a real estate agent that only has his picture and phone number, I throw it away. However, if he sends me something of value, I will put it on my refrigerator. What if you order magnets with your name and business information that also have a place to insert a picture with a message that says something like "The apple of my eye"? Now your magnet is going to go on your client's refrigerator, and when friends and family visit, your client is going to show them his or her grandchildren's picture—with your name and contact information in plain view. Referrals will come your way.

PROFITABILITY

Profitability is the third pillar of your agency. We are in business to make money and provide for our families. Sometimes, agents make the mistake of thinking that just because their agency doesn't physically pay for a claim, their agency is not going to be impacted. Many carriers offer profit bonuses to ensure that agents will pre-underwrite the risks before binding coverage. If your losses are over the threshold stipulated to receive the bonus, your agency loses the bonus. In addition, if your losses continue to be over the threshold, the carrier may eventually terminate the agency contract. You must run a profitable agency.

Reducing and managing your claims will have a great impact on your profitability.

Now you have the pillars of your business: bringing in good customers by creating and adhering to a sound marketing plan, retaining them through excellence in customer service, and maintaining a growing and profitable agency while maximizing your bonuses.

Before we finish this chapter, I want to bring to your attention a law that was first discovered in 1897 by an Italian economist, Vilfredo Pareto (1848–1923). This law impacts your agency in a direct way. Since it was discovered, it has become known as the 80/20 Principle, the Pareto Principle, the Pareto Law, the Principle of Least Effort, and the Principle of Imbalance. The principle states that there is an imbalance between inputs and outputs, focus and results. The principle impacts your agency with the knowledge that, on average, 20 percent of your employees' work brings 80 percent of the results; 20 percent of your clients bring 80 percent of the income; 20 percent of your clients bring 80 percent of the work; etc.

With that knowledge, which you can confirm just by doing a bit of research in your agency, you can make changes in your operation that can bring an impact in an incredible way. The first place to start is to run a report of all your clients and sort them by premium, starting with the largest premium first. Those clients are the ones bringing you the best revenue. If the Pareto Principle applies to your agency, you may find that 20 percent of the clients will bring 80 percent of the income. The next step is to communicate who those customers are to your staff. Those customers need to become a priority of attention and service in your agency. Some agency management systems allow you to classify your customers. If you can, use technology to identify these customers.

A problem that happens regularly in our industry and with which we, as managers, are very aware is the following: A phone call comes in from a customer. He has some billing issues that must be dealt with or else you lose the customer. The employee takes the information, calls the carrier, investigates the problem, understands the solution, calls the customer, and collects the payment. This process may take a good part of two hours. In the meantime, two other phone calls come in with quote requests for home and auto packages that the employee could not answer since she was very involved in the billing problem. Another quote for a package that was on her desk didn't get done because the phone rang with the billing problem and an irate customer. After you look more closely into this problem, you find out that the customer with the billing problem is a customer that is chronically late on his payments, thus the billing issues, and only has one auto insured with your agency. Since you didn't specify to your employee the priorities of her job description, your agency lost three potential packages worth more than the customer she was trying to help. Identifying your customers will help take care of this problem. In addition, your agency performance will become more efficient if you take the time to do the next exercise.

The next step is to analyze every job description in your office. You must have job descriptions for each one of your employees if you want to be efficient. As you look at every area in a job description, try as best as you can to put a percentage value next to the task that would identify that particular task according to how much time your employee spends on it on a daily basis. For this exercise, you need your employee's input. When you finish, the total of all the tasks must equal to 100%. If a certain employee does some tasks that can only be measured on a weekly basis, such as a task like scanning that can take a whole day of the week, the best way to measure that employee's job description is weekly. This study will give you a good idea how each employee's time is spent.

The next step is for you, as agency principal or manager, to put a percentage value next to each task according to the level of importance as you see it. You will end up with 100%. Some tasks you will have given a 5 percent importance and other will have 20 percent.

To complete this study, you will realign all the tasks according to their importance, with the highest being on the top. On a separate area, you will also realign all the tasks according to how much time the employee spends on them.

Compare both studies. The best result is the one where your employee spends most of the time on the tasks that you see as most important. You may be surprised to see that for some employees, or for all of them, 80 percent of their time is spent on areas that you gave only 20 percent importance. If you make the necessary changes, you will improve your agency's efficiency exponentially. The first positive impact will come just with the communication to your employees of their tasks according to importance. The effect of this exercise comes in multiple ways. For example, by your employees focusing on the important tasks, some of the urgent, crisis situations will be avoided. Your operation will become proactive as opposed to reactive.

For copies of charts that will help you evaluate your employee's tasks according to importance and time spent, click on the Resources tab at the book's Web site: www. TheInsuranceProfession.com.

Before I finish this chapter, I want to introduce you to another tool of management that will help you achieve your goals. It is called "perceptual maps." I have used perceptual maps on several occasions as a tool to help me understand different levels of communication. I have found them to be a very good tool.

A perceptual map is based on the fact that perception is reality. You may have the best agency operation in the world, but if your customers do not perceive your agency that way, their perception is reality. They will leave your agency. You can be the best employer, but if your employees do not perceive it that way, their perception is reality. They will look for another job.

Perception is a very powerful thing. That is why the politicians running for office try so hard to build that positive, hardworking perception for the public while trying to damage the perception that the public has of others.

How do we know what perception our employees have of us, our agency operation?

How about our customers? If you don't know what impression they have of you and your agency, all your efforts to service your customers better, as well as becoming a better employer, may be futile. How do you know what you need to change? That is why "perceptual maps" are so very important.

In order to get a good reading of this tool, you must design the perceptual maps based on the information you want to gather. Let's start with your employees. Things you may want to measure are the perception of your pay scale in comparison with other jobs in the same industry, team atmosphere, perception about your management skills, and the organization of the agency.

Visit www.TheInsuranceProfession.com and click on the Resources tab. You will find two perceptual maps that you can use as a tool to get feedback from your employees. There is a vertical line with a plus on the right and a minus on the left. The vertical line is called "Pay Scale." If an employee chooses to the right of the middle, he will believe that he is underpaid. The diamond on the middle will mean that the perception is that your agency pays average, and the diamond on the right will show a pay scale above average. On the Work Atmosphere map, I show a diamond as an example. The example diamond shows that the employee wants to communicate with you that the pay scale is below average but the benefits are above average.

This message is very important to you. If someone believes that your pay scale is below average and your benefits are below average, you will not be able to keep employees. Don't be confused; not every employee will always feel that he is underpaid. In addition, benefits have a much larger value that we, as managers, believe. For instance, flexibility for a mom to be able to leave work because of an emergency with her child will have great value when considering the package you offer between pay scale and bene-fits. If employers do not know how their employees feel, they will continue to invest in new employ-ees only to lose them to the competition, which not only will benefit from a trained employee but will also learn your successful processes.

In order for this tool to be effective, you must do the exercise and have every one of your employees do his or hers. Don't ask them to put their names on the chart. In order for this information to be accurate, you must respect their anonymity. When you gather all the results, compare the results with your per-ception. If the majority of the maps don't line up, the larger the discrepancy, the more work you are going to have to do. For example, if you believe you are paying above average and most of your employees perceive your pay to be below average, there is some work you have to do. This doesn't always mean that you have to give them a raise. Perhaps you need to work on the perception that your employees have of the benefits that you provide.

On the Web site you will also find another perceptual map called Management Style. The example diamond here shows that your employees perceive you as a micromanager, but once they understand what you want from them, they all pull together to get the job done. The teamwork is very positive; they all have learned how to communicate and work as a team to accomplish your goals. The negative part is that they view you as a micromanager, someone who doesn't delegate projects but has to be involved to control every step of the project. You may not view yourself as a micromanager, but if the majority of your employees see you that way, you have to make some changes.

Now that I believe you understand the concept, I want to review the process one more time. You communicate with your employees that you want to evaluate your agency and would like their input. Your employees will appreciate that. Give each one of them a copy of each of the perceptual maps. Tell them not to write their names. You are interested in the data, not the source. You take the time to also take a map and complete the exercise yourself. Once everyone is done, compare the results from the employees with your maps. This will give you the understanding of how your employees perceive you. Remember that perception is reality. Make the necessary changes to change the perception the way you want. Create your own perceptual maps to obtain the information that you need, and do it once every year to see if any changes happened.

Now that you know how this tool works, you can design some perceptual maps for your customers based on the information you want to receive from them. This tool will improve your agency from the employee side and from the customer side.

CHAPTER 11

Taking Your Agency
to the Next Level

Perfection is not when there is no
more to add, but no more to take away.

ANTOINE DE SAINT-EXUPERY
Pioneer of international postal flight

I was talking to a gentleman that I met at a conference. We were talking about insurance (of course), and I asked him how long he had been with his agent. He told me it had been eighteen years. I said, "You must really like your agent to have him look after your assets that long. He must be a good friend by now." He replied that he had never met him, but that every time he called his office, the agent returned the call within twenty-four hours. I have found this to be more the norm than the exception: agents who not only don't know their clients well but aren't making sure to keep up with their changing needs and exposures.

Answer this question: how can clients trust someone they have never met to protect their assets? Clients make additions to their homes, purchase art, inherit valuable collectibles, and purchase trampolines and other toys for their children that expose their family's liability. They install pools without fences, buy dangerous or exotic pets, and they need guidance to protect themselves. The industry needs insurance agents who take the time to know their clients and understand their lifestyle changes. If we consider ourselves merely salespeople, we are missing what this industry is all about. I have walked into insurance offices that look like insurance depots: multiple desks all lined up with agents cranking out insurance policies for strangers like they were working on an assembly line. Many people in this industry sell insurance like any other tangible product. I don't mean to offend you if you are currently running that type of operation, but I want to tell you that this type of operation will not have much of a future.

Our profession is asset management. In order to protect our client's assets, we use insurance products, but remember that in order to find the best product that fits the client's needs we need to first understand those needs. Relationships are at the heart of what we do. We sell insurance based on the trust placed in us. We, as insurance professionals, do not sell insurance policies to protect merely assets; we sell insurance policies to protect our client's *lifestyles*.

Unfortunately, the reputation of the insurance business has been marred by far too many uncaring agents who are only looking to close a sale. Clients have come to expect that when they call their agent's office, the only thing they'll get is a recording. They go to visit their agent, and he is not there. They get a rate increase with no warning from the agent before the bill arrives. Their insurance lapses for the first time in years, and the agent lets the insurance cancel, leaving them exposed to lose everything.

Friend, we cannot treat our clients poorly and expect them to stay with us for long. The gentleman I spoke of earlier, who had stayed with a virtual stranger for eighteen years, is a rarity. Not long ago, the only concern was losing a client to another agent, but when a person has a poor understanding of what an agent can and should be doing on his behalf, he's likely to believe that all agents are the same. This person could easily be swayed by the barrage of television commercials wooing customers to shop *online*. I must say here that many disgruntled insurance customers are on the verge of rebellion. They are dissatisfied with our services, and although they may stay with a neglectful agent for a while, it won't take much to get them to move their business. Why do you think online insurance sales are increasing at dramatic proportions every day? If we sell insurance like any other product, the consumer is going to buy insurance like any other product— online. Clients cannot buy asset management online, but they are getting used to buying just about any product online with the perception that it will save them money. Consumers are being trained to leave out what they consider the "middleman" and go straight to the source with the click of a mouse.

As agents, we need to work hard and move fast if we want to retain our customers and our business. We must bring value to our customers if we want to retain them. Remember your *value proposition*? I need to reiterate: you must know it; your staff must know it; you must post it all over your office and include it in every piece of mail you send to your customers. That is the line that you want your customers to use when they think of your business and refer you to others. That is what sets you apart from the rest of the agents or online sales, but remember that once you publish your value proposition, you have to live up to it!

CLOSING
THOUGHTS

I have shared with you as a friend most of what I have learned during my years in the insurance industry. My last message to you is that we, the insurance agents, must provide a unified front in order to continue to lead the industry. As I have shared with many of you, I have detected that many of you see each other as the competition. We have been secretive with each other with the intention of protecting our businesses, but that can't continue.

The industry is changing before our eyes, and we must shift our perspective to reflect what is happening in the industry today. The other agents around you, whether captive or independent, are not your direct competition. The markets that are growing at dramatic proportions are the direct markets, offered by carriers and conglomerates like insureme.com, esurance.com, etc. Financial institutions and associations such as home loan companies associated with home builders are also getting a good portion of the market.

Not long ago the only choice the consumer had was which

> If the only thing you sell is price, why does a carrier need you?

carrier to go with. Then the independent agent came along with a variety of carriers to offer, and many captive agents saw clients leaving in droves. And now, the new power player is the cold, uncaring computer, with promises of low prices and hassle-free claims, yet nothing in the way of true value or concern. The main differ-ence is in the quality service that comes from a personal relationship and the value proposi-tion that you bring to the table. If you ever find yourself more concerned about selling insur-ance based on price alone, and not focusing on protecting the lifestyle of your clients, you run the very real risk of losing them. If the only thing that you sell is price, why does a carrier need you?

We, as agents, must create a unified front to help each other raise the bar. We must sharpen our skills and repair our reputation so that clients will want to purchase protection for their families and their assets through us.

I hope the reading of these pages have been an inspiration to you so that you may become better at our profession.

Thank you for taking the time to read the thoughts and experiences conveyed here.

Tony Fernandez

Appendix A

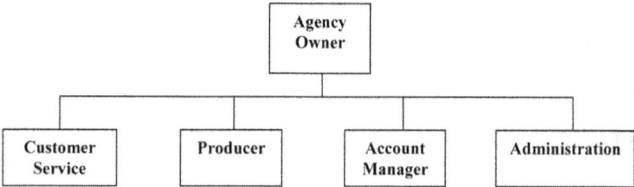

Appendix B

Scenario: The total amount of commissions that you receive in a given month is $18,000.

Total amount received by carrier: $18,000

    Personal lines: $13,000

    Commercial lines: $5,000

Personal Lines

Total employee hours: 516 x $14 (average hourly rate including taxes) = **$7,224**

Cost per employee hour is: **55%** (for every $100 that the agency receives, you have to pay **$55** in employee costs)

Commercial Lines

Total employee hours: 344 x $14 (average hourly rate including taxes) = **$4,816**

Cost per employee hour is: **96%** (for every $100 that the agency receives, you have to pay **$96** in employee costs)

In this particular scenario, you can see that the most profitable line for your agency is personal lines. You have to make some significant changes in commercial lines to increase the profitability. Both lines should function with the same index per employee cost.

Glossary Of Terms

Direct Writer – An insurance carrier who distributes its products via an insurance agent who can only sell the direct writer products.

Captive Agent – An agent who is contracted to sell products from a Direct Writer

Master Code – The main number assigned to an insurance agent to authorize the representation of an insurance carrier

Errors And Omissions – The insurance coverage that insurance agents need to protect their practice.